50
STEPS
FORWARD

Bible readings and prayers
for 50 days

Published by the Torch Trust for the Blind

TORCH

50 STEPS FORWARD

First published in Great Britain 2009 by Torch Trust for the Blind;
Torch House, Torch Way, Market Harborough, Leicestershire
LE16 9HL; tel: 01858 438260; fax: 01858 438275;
email: info@torchtrust.org; website: www.torchtrust.org
The Torch Trust for the Blind, registered charity no: 1095904

ISBN 978-0-9515851-5-3

Compilation and additional material by Lydia Tebbutt; edited by Lin Ball

Cover and internal page design by Ranieri Figueiredo; cover photographs by Paul Ferraby www.paulferraby.co.uk

Printed and bound by Nuffield Press, Abingdon, England
www.nuffield.co.uk

50 STEPS FORWARD

Bible readings and prayers
for 50 days

CONTENTS

BEGINNINGS

The work of Torch Trust began with a simple act of kindness. Ron and Stella Heath, living with their family in Reigate, Surrey, UK, loved to open their home to young people. Ron ran activities for a group of teenage boys, so Stella began a club for girls – the 'Friday nighters'. One of the girls, Lillian, worked as a cook at a training centre for blind people. One day she asked if she could bring a blind girl to the club. Stella agreed.

As Stella afterwards recalled, 'I had no idea how much hard work, disrupted home life, tears and heartache that reply would lead to. Nor did I know the joys, triumphs and the sheer gladness of serving the Lord that would come our way because of the advent of blind people into our lives.'

So 18-year-old Wendy came to tea. Wendy had been blind since birth. She'd had two operations, could see nothing out of her left eye and just had a small amount of vision in her right. She listened to the talks and joined in the singing of hymns. Three weeks later she prayed to receive Jesus Christ as her Lord.

The change in Wendy's life was quickly noticed by the principal of the training centre, who wondered if the Heaths could help others. And that's how a large group of blind young men and women started turning up regularly for Sunday tea at the Heaths' home. A number of them, like Wendy, decided to become Christians.

Ron and Stella Heath developed empathy for the young blind people they met and had a real desire to share their Christian faith with them. They became concerned about how blind people could read the Bible and other Christian books, and were strongly challenged by the words of Jesus to the disciples when faced with the hungry five thousand: 'You give them something to eat.' They discovered there was a Christian magazine for people with sight loss, started in 1931, called *The Torch*, produced by some elderly sisters in the north of England. They began to learn braille themselves and to recruit others for the task of transcribing. The work with blind people not only took over their home but their lives and certainly their hearts.

On June 8, 1959, the Heaths formally took over *The Torch* magazine and the trust formed by the Trench sisters. Fifty years later, Torch Trust, still providing Christian literature and fellowship for blind and partially sighted people, has around 40 staff supported by more than a thousand volunteers, and its magazines are distributed in 100 countries.

And it all started the day Ron and Stella Heath invited Wendy to tea...

KEY DATES IN
TORCH TRUST HISTORY

1958	Ron and Stella Heath invite blind young people to their home
1959	The Heaths take over *The Torch* magazine; Torch Trust founded; Gladstone Moore becomes the first chair of trustees
1962	Torch Trust growth leads to move to house in Crawley, Sussex
1964	First Torch houseparty held at a hotel in Crawley
1968	Torch Trust growth leads to move to first Torch House at Hurstpierpoint, Sussex
1970	First Torch Fellowship Group founded in Birmingham
1974	Torch Trust growth leads to move to house in Hallaton, Leicestershire
1976	International conference of Christian ministries to blind people, hosted by Torch, held at Hallaton
1985	Ray Adams becomes chair of trustees
1989	Stella Heath and Rosina Sharp visit Africa
1991	Founding of Torch Trust for the Blind International (Malawi)
1992	International conference of Christian ministries to blind people, hosted by Torch, held at Hothorpe Hall
1998	Ron Wells becomes chair of trustees
1999	Death of Ron Heath
2002	Dr Gordon Temple becomes CEO
2004	New purpose-built production centre and offices open at Torch House, Market Harborough, Leicestershire
2008	Marilyn Baker becomes chair of trustees
2009	Death of Stella Heath Torch Trust celebrates its 50th anniversary

50 STEPS FORWARD –
AN ANNIVERSARY CELEBRATION

from Torch Trust CEO Dr Gordon Temple

50 **STEPS FORWARD** is a book to encourage Bible reading and prayer – two Christian disciplines which have been foundational throughout the history of Torch Trust. At Torch House, each day starts with Bible reading and prayer, with everyone gathered in the conference room. Prayer is offered for staff, volunteers, people with sight loss we have contact with throughout the UK and around the world, fellowship groups, publishing projects, events and holidays, financial needs. As it says in our *Daily Prayer Guide* produced for supporters: 'Prayer connects us with our heavenly Father, with his insight, foresight and resources. Without it we hardly dare do anything in his service; with it we can do anything that is in line with his perfect will.'

As you take up this book we want to ask you to set out on a 50-day adventure of prayer and Bible reading – to give praise and thanksgiving to the God who has blessed Torch so wonderfully; to seek God's will with us for the next 50 years of Torch ministry; and to bless you personally. What will Torch Trust look like in another half century? With God's help, we feel compelled to grow our work to touch the lives of thousands more blind and partially sighted people.

The book models in many respects the kind of movement we try to be, especially in its inclusivity. The comment material here has been written by a wide range of contributors – by people who are blind and sighted, by famous and little known, by professionals and those with few worldly skills, by people from different ethnic backgrounds – all of whom were invited to choose a verse or passage on a given theme which had some significance to them. All age groups are represented, including one contributor as young as twelve. Some of those who have willingly written for this book have served or continue to serve Torch as staff, trustees or volunteers; others receive Torch services. The prayers and reflections have been added by Torch editorial staff. The book is being produced simultaneously in braille, giant print and audio formats.

Fifty years is a noteworthy milestone for a number of reasons. In the Jewish calendar there are 50 days between the Sabbath (Saturday) of the Passover weekend and Pentecost – the festival of harvest or first fruits. We think of these times more commonly as Easter and Whitsun.

This period, stretching from the death and burial of Jesus through to the coming of the Holy Spirit, was a difficult time for the early followers of Jesus. When he talked to his closest followers before his death, Jesus warned them of the tough times ahead. But they just didn't get it!

The outrageously unjust crucifixion of Jesus shattered their hopes, leaving them shell-shocked and bewildered. At first, the resurrection appearances of their Master confused as much as excited them. For want of something better to do, Peter returned to the family business – fishing (John 21). And just when they might be getting used to the idea of Jesus still being around, he told them he was leaving – for good – and disappeared before their very eyes!

Then there was a time of waiting. And finally, when 120 followers were huddled together, the promised Holy Spirit broke in dramatically and the explosive growth of the global Church began. Now they understood!

We all go through times of confusion, bewilderment, waiting and even doubt. The words of Jesus can seem irrelevant to our circumstances. We need help.

Our prayer is that as you follow this series of readings you will once again experience the in-breaking of God's Spirit, bringing a fresh helping of life and vigour, blowing away doubt and confusion, and lighting within you a fire of passion to serve God. After all, the Holy Spirit brings to us the potential to change the world!

HOW TO USE
50 STEPS FORWARD

from Torch Literature Leader Lydia Tebbutt

Each week of material in this book has its own THEME, explained in an introduction. Each day's material consists of a BIBLE READING chosen on the theme by a guest writer, together with their comments. Sometimes more than one contributor has chosen the same verses, but the comments have always been different. The editor Lin Ball and I have added some thoughts to help you REFLECT on the Bible verses and see how they might speak to your situation or impact your life; and also given opportunities for you to PRAY and PRAISE God. I would encourage you to use the prayers as a springboard for your own; what is given is not intended to be prescriptive but to free you to express yourself in your relationship with God.

Often we have suggested using a PHYSICAL OBJECT which you may find helpful in focusing and giving a fresh dimension to your prayer thoughts. This 'multi-sensory' approach means that prayer is not limited to an activity of the mind or simply to words. Prayer and praise can be enhanced by touch, taste, hearing, sight or smell – particularly as we engage with the physical world that God has created.

This 'MULTI-SENSORY' approach has particular value where a person has lost one of their senses, but the benefits can be felt by anyone. If you would like to further explore this – either as an individual or in the setting of a small group or within the wider Church – we commend to you the published range of 'Multi-Sensory' resource books from Scripture Union (www.scriptureunion.org.uk).

May the Lord speak to you as you draw near to him and bless you as you journey with us through **50 STEPS FORWARD.**

PRAYER

Itinerant evangelist John Wesley famously wrote, 'I have so much to do that I must spend several hours in prayer before I am able to do it.' Any busy charity HQ is likely to forget the need for prayer when phone calls and emails are to be answered, visitors are to be taken care of, production deadlines are to be met. But the work of Torch Trust has a heritage of prayer, and staff continue to remind themselves daily that '**Unless the Lord builds the house, the builders labour in vain**' **(Psalm 127:1).**

> **Prayer is the most important thing in my life.**
> **If I should neglect prayer for a single day,**
> **I should lose a great deal of the fire of faith.**
>
> **– German church reformer Martin Luther**

ENCOURAGEMENT

'It was towards the end of the summer of 1976 … Prices were rather higher than usual for food and, as is often the case in the summer, we were not getting enough gifts to cover expenses. We had begun to learn to pray believing that God would answer. So we prayed for the Lord to prompt people to send us the money we needed.

'Then one morning John Oldham came into the kitchen with something in his hands – some of the biggest, juiciest mushrooms you could imagine! And there were plenty more on the lawn. Every day for a fortnight we had a rich supply of mushrooms! The Lord did supply the money eventually, but he taught us that he could answer prayer in the most unexpected ways sometimes … And do you know? We have never had mushrooms growing on the lawn like that since!'

From Coping with the Camel (1996) *by* Stella Heath

> **The purpose of all prayer is to find God's will and to make that will our prayer.**
>
> *– inspirational American writer Catherine Marshall*

'When our high-speed braille embosser goes wrong, one or other of the Torch staff can usually identify and fix the problem – but not this time! ... Naturally we prayed – a lot! The work was piling up – thousands of braille magazines awaited by blind readers all over the world. So we asked our friends at the RNIB if they could help, knowing that their production schedules were usually very tight. We were delighted when they said they could produce our magazines the very next week. But it didn't stop there. Our production team was invited to visit and were offered any technical assistance we might need in the future. We all realised the truth that our God is able to do abundantly, exceedingly more than we can ever dream or ask for.

April 2009, Torch staff member

> **You need not cry very loud; he is nearer to us than we think.**
>
> *– Brother Lawrence, author of*
> **The Practice of the Presence of God**

MULTI-SENSORY FOCUS

As you spend time with God in prayer and praise this coming week, have a bunch of keys with you. A key is not only a wonderfully useful object in itself, but the idea of a key can lead to all kinds of possibilities. As an ordinary piece of metal it's simply a tool to fit into a lock or draw a bolt. But we also talk of a key as being anything that enables us to enter an experience or access something, as in 'the key to happiness'. Or it can express something vital, as in 'the key to solving the mystery'. How is prayer like a key? What might prayer unlock for you?

THIS WEEK'S CONTRIBUTORS

HEATHER WILLIAMS • GEMMA GARDNER • REV'D HELEN PATTEN • MICHAEL STAFFORD • BRIDGET NAYLOR • TRACY WILLIAMSON • SUSAN POTTER

PRAYER: Our Father in heaven

MATTHEW 6:6–13   I PETER 5:7

… when you pray, go into your room, close the door and pray to your Father, who is unseen. Then your Father, who sees what is done in secret, will reward you…

This, then, is how you should pray:

'Our Father in heaven, hallowed be your name, your kingdom come, your will be done, on earth as it is in heaven. Give us today our daily bread. And forgive us our debts, as we also have forgiven our debtors. And lead us not into temptation, but deliver us from the evil one.'

HEATHER WILLIAMS WRITES

Consider this awakening to God in prayer from the hymn writer James Montgomery: 'Prayer is the soul's sincere desire, uttered, or unexpressed.'

To have communication with our heavenly God and Father as Jesus did himself and as he taught his disciples, can be the most wonderful expression of our love for him and our thankfulness for our salvation.

Jesus teaches us in this passage how to pray privately, pointedly and with purpose – and the Father will reward us. What matters as we pray is that we pray what we feel in heart and spirit. As Jesus teaches elsewhere, we are to seek first his kingdom and his will, but we can also ask for our daily needs to be met.

Forgiving others as we ask forgiveness for ourselves is vital – otherwise we are in danger of harbouring bitter thoughts and resentments.

We also ask God to keep us from temptation. On two other occasions (Luke 22:40,46) Jesus refers to the possibility of us falling into temptation, so this must be very important.

Jesus doesn't only teach about prayer but sets an example. Take, for example, Matthew 14. Knowing that his cousin John the Baptist has just been beheaded, Jesus wants to go somewhere. But the crowds follow him and need to be fed. A miracle takes place as more than five thousand are fed. After dismissing the crowd, Jesus then goes up the mountain to be solitary and pray. In the midst of his busy life, Jesus makes time to seek his Father's face. What a wonderful example for us to follow! He practised what he taught.

The sending of the Holy Spirit after the death and resurrection of Jesus provides us with extra encouragement to pray as we continue to work for the kingdom of God. So let us be prepared to pray – and expect results.

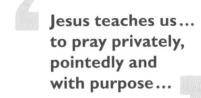

**Jesus teaches us...
to pray privately,
pointedly and
with purpose...**

REFLECT

Take the bunch of keys in your hand and think about what might be the key to understanding the Lord's Prayer. Think about each phrase and what it means for you at this point in your life. As you come to a new phrase, take a single key between your fingers and don't let go of it until you have asked yourself, 'What does this mean for me, right now?' and come to some kind of answer. Move on to another key, and another phrase. If unresolved issues come to mind, ask God to show you if you are to take any action, or simply trust God to work it out for you. How challenging it is to see how completely Jesus lived out his teaching!

PRAISE

I praise and thank you, Father God, for the gift of prayer which means personal closeness to you.

PRAY

Lord, as you have provided so generously for Torch over 50 years, please continue to give the 'daily bread' needed for its work with blind and partially sighted people. Amen.

ABOUT HEATHER WILLIAMS

For 20 years Heather worked for RNIB; then in 1987 she began working for Torch, first as a housekeeper at the house at Hallaton and then in the tape library. Although officially retired, Heather works four mornings a week in Library Administration. She also records Bible readings for the audio version of *Every Day with Jesus*, sings with the Torch Singers, and serves as a trustee.

PRAYER: The answer to anxiety

PHILIPPIANS 4:6,7; 1 PETER 5:7

Do not be anxious about anything, but in every situation, by prayer and petition, with thanksgiving, present your requests to God. And the peace of God, which transcends all understanding, will guard your hearts and your minds in Christ Jesus.

... Cast all your anxiety on him because he cares for you.

GEMMA GARDNER WRITES

What a challenge these words are in these times of uncertainty! I still struggle in this area of trusting God and not worrying. The opposite of anxiety is trust – and Jesus is our perfect example of trust. When he was on earth, he trusted his Father totally to take care of him. In his Sermon on the Mount, Jesus said, '... your Father knows what you need before you ask him' (Matthew 6:8).

When we put our trust in Jesus to save us from our sins, we enter into a new relationship with him. He has opened the way for us to come to God, and we can truly say that God is our Father. But we can only grow in our relationship with God as we come to him in prayer. He is the perfect Father and wants the best for us. He longs that we bring all our anxieties and needs to him. He wants to be involved in every part of our lives. No problem is too big or too trivial for him to solve and, as we thank him for his answers, our trust will grow. We are able to look back and see how he has answered our prayers and led us in our daily lives.

Are you feeling anxious today? God cares for you. Bring your worries to him in prayer and trust him to answer! He will never fail nor forsake you.

PRAISE

*I praise you, Lord, for your
peace, which is truly beyond
human understanding and
which protects me from feeling
overwhelmed by anxieties.
Thank you, too, that no difficulty
I face is greater than your
love and concern for me.*

REFLECT

Today, let your keys represent the
keys to freedom from worry and
anxiety. Hold them tightly in your
hand. Then re-read the verses
from Philippians out loud and, as
you do so, gradually release your
fingers from around the keys. As
you reach the end, drop the keys
into your lap as a sign of releasing
your anxieties to God.

PRAY

*Father, many people who are
losing their sight are troubled
with all kinds of worries,
especially about their future.
May they come to know and
trust you; and may many
of them discover practical
help and emotional support
through coming into contact
with Torch Trust. Amen.*

ABOUT GEMMA GARDNER

Gemma Gardner was born blind in October 1952. She gained some
sight in one eye following several operations. Her childhood was
difficult and she spent four of her teenage years in various psychiatric
institutions. Things changed for the better when she gave her life to
Christ during a visit to Torch House in August 1970. She worked at
Torch from 1974 to 1990. She married in 2003 and now lives in Norwich.
Gemma continues to be in touch with Torch and is involved with
helping on the Torch 'Searchlight' magazine.

PRAYER: Into God's hands

JOHN 2:1–3,6–10

On the third day a wedding took place at Cana in Galilee. Jesus' mother was there, and Jesus and his disciples had also been invited to the wedding. When the wine was gone, Jesus' mother said to him, 'They have no more wine.'

… Nearby stood six stone water jars…

Jesus said to the servants, 'Fill the jars with water'; so they filled them to the brim.

Then he told them, 'Now draw some out and take it to the master of the banquet.'

They did so, and the master of the banquet tasted the water that had been turned into wine. He did not realise where it had come from, though the servants who had drawn the water knew. Then he called the bridegroom aside and said, 'Everyone brings out the choice wine first and then the cheaper wine after the guests have had too much to drink; but you have saved the best till now.'

HELEN PATTEN WRITES

At first glance, this passage isn't about prayer at all. But look more closely and Mary will teach us something very simple but most essential about what we need to do when we pray.

There is a serious problem: a wedding is being celebrated, wine has run out, and the guests could soon become bad-tempered and critical. Mary instinctively knows what to do: she brings the problem to Jesus – not suggesting various things that he might do, but just placing the matter firmly in his hands. Children naturally do this all the time: 'Mum, I've spilt something down my jumper!' 'Dad, the chain's come off my bike!' They trust that their parents will know exactly what to do for the best.

Similarly, when we pray we are not giving God advice or telling him what to do – he has

> **Placing our concerns in God's hands as we pray is … the beginning of a transforming adventure**

far more loving wisdom and understanding than we shall ever have – but just placing the person, the situation, the crisis in his entirely capable hands. This makes praying a very restful and burden-relieving experience because, humanly speaking, we often don't know what we should ask or how a particular problem could ever be resolved. Yet through prayer we have the privilege of bringing these matters to a loving Father whose thoughts and ways are much higher than ours, and who has the power to do things far beyond our imagining.

Mary, of course, had no idea how Jesus would tackle the need which she brought to him, but she was utterly certain that he would respond and that whatever he did would bring blessing. And so it is for us. Placing our concerns in God's hands as we pray is never the end of the story, but rather the beginning of a transforming adventure.

REFLECT

Use your keys to remind you of problems that need unlocking. Be honest to God about your inability to come up with answers or resolutions. Transfer the keys from one hand to the other as you name before God the issues that come to mind. If you know it, you could sing the song, 'Father, I place into your hands the things I cannot do.'

PRAISE

I praise you, Lord, for the way you have met the needs of Torch Trust for over half a century, often miraculously providing 'wine' when supplies were exhausted.

PRAY

I ask that all those involved in the work of Torch will seek and embrace your extraordinary and perfect solution to every problem and challenge. Amen.

ABOUT HELEN PATTEN

After teaching in mainstream schools for eleven years, Helen Patten was ordained as a minister in the Church of England. Having served in parishes in Kent, Sussex and Derbyshire, she then spent over five years as chaplain of St Michael's Hospice in Hastings. Helen, who has been completely without sight since birth, has been married to Michael for over 20 years. In retirement her relaxations include walking and wildlife, choral singing, making bread and entertaining friends.

PRAYER: Wherever we are

JONAH 2:1–3,6,7

From inside the fish Jonah prayed to the LORD his God. He said:

> 'In my distress I called to the LORD,
> and he answered me.
> From deep in the realm of the dead I called for help,
> and you listened to my cry.
>
> 'You hurled me into the deep,
> into the very heart of the seas,
> and the currents swirled about me;
> all your waves and breakers
> swept over me.
>
> … 'To the roots of the mountains I sank down;
> the earth beneath barred me in forever.
> But you, LORD my God,
> brought my life up from the pit.
>
> 'When my life was ebbing away,
> I remembered you, LORD,
> and my prayer rose to you,
> to your holy temple.'

MICHAEL STAFFORD WRITES

Jonah was probably the only person ever to have prayed to God from inside a fish! Yet his action illustrates the fact that we can pray to God from any location, in any situation. The only instruction we have in the New Testament as to the best place to pray is in Matthew 6:6: 'But when you pray, go into your room, close the door and pray to your Father, who is unseen.' And we should 'pray continually' (1 Thessalonians 5:17), which means at any time of the day or night, wherever we may be.

This Bible passage also reminds us that an extreme situation, such as that in which Jonah found himself, often engenders prayer. Many stories are told of mariners who have been in mortal danger in rough seas praying to God for the first time in their lives and experiencing God's deliverance. Often in such circumstances the person in danger makes promises to God – if only he will deliver them! Sometimes these promises have been kept, and lives have been committed to God and his service.

Does God answer prayer? Yes – but not always with a 'yes'! Sometimes the answer will be 'no' or 'wait'. God, in his infinite wisdom, knows what's best for us, or the one we are praying for. He can see what we can't.

> **God, in his infinite wisdom, knows what's best for us, or the one we are praying for**

He knows what we are able to do and what we must leave to others to do. In Jonah's case, God had further work for him to do, and therefore his answer was 'yes'. And Jonah was miraculously delivered from a watery grave.

REFLECT

Where will you be spending time this week? Where might you be travelling? Where is God sending you? As you pick up the bunch of keys, think of all the places you expect to visit – your home, your workplace, the church, the post office, a friend's home. Ask God to make you aware of his presence in each different place, to bless your time there and to bless the people you will meet.

PRAISE

I praise you, Lord God, for all the places where I am welcome, and all the relationships those places represent.

PRAY

I pray for the whole Torch family to experience the reality of knowing a God who is near in all circumstances and who answers prayer. Amen.

ABOUT MICHAEL STAFFORD

Michael is a printer by trade. He took a Bible college course before going to serve the Lord in Christian literature and Bible teaching in Nigeria for 17 years. This was followed by six years managing a Christian conference centre before becoming involved with Torch Trust in the days when it was based at Hallaton, mainly working in the areas of giant print and braille production. Michael is keenly involved along with his wife Janet in Torch ministry in Malawi. He has been with Torch for 22 years. He and Janet have two children and four grandchildren.

PRAYER: God is near

PSALM 145:17–21

The LORD is righteous in all his ways
and faithful in all he does.

The LORD is near to all who call on him,
to all who call on him in truth.

He fulfils the desires of those who fear him;
he hears their cry and saves them.

The LORD watches over all who love him,
but all the wicked he will destroy.

My mouth will speak in praise of the LORD.
Let every creature praise his holy name
for ever and ever.

BRIDGET NAYLOR WRITES

Prayer, at its very basic level, is engaging with God – being yourself before him. It's communicating our thoughts and desires to someone in whose character we have complete trust.

'Do something!' was the sum total of one of my first honest prayers to God. I was engaging with God in the only way I could at the time. It didn't matter that it wasn't a long prayer, but to reach God's heart it did have to be genuine. God is watching over all who love him and he can hear the cry of our hearts. I called out to God in truth and he drew near to me. I was able to be real because I had experienced the gift of salvation

> God hears, God draws near, and God enters into our concerns as we cry out to him

and had some idea of who God was. I was growing in awareness of how awesome and great God was. Secure in this knowledge, I had no hesitation in being completely open with him.

My simple prayer was a response to all that was in my heart, with the expectancy that he would hear and draw near. As I prayed I allowed God into my situation. I was able to see that God is righteous and faithful in all his dealings with me.

God hears, God draws near, and God enters into our concerns as we cry out to him. Through prayer, wonderfully, we connect with the Almighty and All-knowing God!

PRAISE

Faithful God, it's so wonderful to be able to trust you completely! I want to live in the assurance and security of that today and every day. Thank you, Father, that you hear my cry when I need you.

REFLECT

Hold the bunch of keys in your hand and picture yourself letting yourself in and out of your own front door. Of course, we know that as we arrive at the door, the key will open it. We have gone in and out of the house many times. We trust our keys to do the task they were designed for. Think about the way God is described in the Bible reading. He is 'righteous … faithful.' He 'is near … he hears … watches over.' Do you trust this loving and faithful God as implicitly as you trust that your key will open your front door?

PRAY

Please draw near to blind and partially sighted people everywhere. Give them opportunities to find out about you and your trustworthiness, and to experience for themselves how you are able to be near to all who call on you, especially through the work of Torch House, Torch Fellowship Groups and the Torch Holiday & Retreat Centre. Amen.

ABOUT BRIDGET NAYLOR

Bridget grew up in Nottingham and became a Christian at the age of 18. She heard about Torch through a blind person in her church and subsequently felt a call from God to join the staff at the house in Hallaton, which she did in 1980. She was responsible for the mailing system on the first computer Torch ever had! In 1994 Bridget moved to work elsewhere. But her sense of belonging to the Torch family never left her heart and she was glad when the way opened for her to return to work for Torch in Market Harborough in 2006 as a braille transcriber.

PRAYER: Hearing God speak

JOHN 15:7,8,15

Jesus said:

'If you remain in me and my words remain in you, ask whatever you wish, and it will be done for you. This is to my Father's glory, that you bear much fruit, showing yourselves to be my disciples.

… 'I no longer call you servants, because servants do not know their master's business. Instead, I have called you friends, for everything that I learned from my Father I have made known to you.'

TRACY WILLIAMSON WRITES

Friendship with God! What a privilege! But what does it really mean?

Jesus desires communication with us. This is the heart of true prayer. We can talk to him knowing that he is interceding on our behalf and he will speak to us as we listen expectantly.

He counsels us even in mundane situations. Recently I caught a bus which headed off in an unexpected direction. I panicked, thinking I'd misread the number. To my surprise, I sensed Jesus saying, 'Relax! It's OK!' Minutes later, the bus turned back; the driver had gone wrong! I was so glad I had listened to Jesus and not jumped off!

> …he will speak to us as we listen expectantly

As a deaf person, conversations with people can be frustrating. But not even our weaknesses can stop us hearing Jesus and praying effectively. I converse with him in my heart, listening for his strategy and wisdom. He may give me insights, by suggesting a Bible verse or an image to my mind. As I trust his guidance and speak it out, I find amazing things happen! Situations are turned around; peace is restored. This shows the power of prayer as conversation with God... not just reciting a list of needs but listening to his heart and praying his purposes.

Once I sensed Jesus saying that a depressed friend was like a fragrant flower. So I daily thanked him for her beauty and fragrance. Soon she began to smile again. I was overjoyed!

Never underestimate your position in Christ and your calling to work in partnership with God in prayer. It will become a life-changing adventure!

PRAISE

I am so grateful, Father, that you always hear me. Thank you for calling me your friend.

REFLECT

Take a key in one hand and use it to trace the shape of an ear on your other palm. Tracy reminds us that prayer is a two way conversation. We need to listen as well as talk. Do you need God to unlock your inner hearing? Are you listening expectantly for his guidance, his insights? Are you asking him how you can bless the people you meet?

PRAY

Help me to listen to you, Lord, so that I can hear from you and your wisdom can have a greater impact in my life. Lord, give listening hearts to all in leadership with Torch, so that the decisions they make are guided by your great wisdom. Amen.

ABOUT TRACY WILLIAMSON

Tracy Williamson works in ministry partnership with Marilyn Baker, offering restoration through music, teaching and prayer. Tracy shares a house with Marilyn in Kent. As a speaker and author of five Christian teaching books, she frequently contributes at Torch events. Living with deafness and sight loss, Tracy is passionate about helping people hear God's voice and experience his love and healing power in their lives. She enjoys travelling; but also loves to spend time at home with friends or relaxing with a good book.

PRAYER: When under threat

2 KINGS 19:14–19

Hezekiah received the letter from the messengers and read it. Then he went up to the temple of the LORD and spread it out before the LORD. And Hezekiah prayed to the LORD: 'LORD, the God of Israel, enthroned between the cherubim, you alone are God over all the kingdoms of the earth. You have made heaven and earth. Give ear, LORD, and hear; open your eyes, LORD, and see; listen to the words Sennacherib has sent to ridicule the living God.

'It is true, LORD, that the Assyrian kings have laid waste these nations and their lands. They have thrown their gods into the fire and destroyed them, for they were not gods but only wood and stone, fashioned by human hands. Now, LORD our God, deliver us from his hand, so that all the kingdoms of the earth may know that you alone, LORD, are God.'

SUSAN POTTER WRITES

Has being a Christian ever got you into hot water? Have you experienced taunts, insults or negative remarks from friends, family, colleagues or classmates because you have spoken about Christ, given a church service priority over something else or tried to take a moral stance? Such negativity can make us feel isolated, or even that we are mistaken in following Christ, and it can sap our spiritual zeal.

King Hezekiah found himself and his people in just such a position. However, it seems that he didn't sit around and mope. Instead, he took it all straight to the Lord and cast it before him. This, of course,

> ...the very best thing to do in all circumstances is to talk to God and listen for his answer

did not take the issue away, but God guided him as to how to deal with the situation. And he'll guide us, too, if we open ourselves to him.

We live in an increasingly intolerant age when it comes to faith in Christ, and we need to cling ever closer to the rock of our salvation.

When things start to get out of perspective, I turn to Hezekiah's prayer, because it reminds me that the very best thing to do in all circumstances is to talk to God and listen for his answer. Laying out my concerns before the Lord as Hezekiah spread out the scroll he received is the best remedy I know for anything; and though God's answers are sometimes difficult, they are always right and given in love.

As the old hymn says:

What a friend we have in Jesus,
All our sins and griefs to bear!
What a privilege to carry
Everything to God in prayer!

REFLECT

Are there any keys in your house tucked away at the back of a drawer because you hardly ever use them? Perhaps there are some 'locked' situations in your life that you've got used to; maybe you can't imagine them ever being 'unlocked'? Prayer can be the key that unlocks even the most difficult circumstances or problems. Why not ask God to help you take everything – yes, everything – to him in prayer right now?

PRAISE

I praise you, Father, that you are so powerful. As Hezekiah discovered, you are 'God over all the kingdoms of the earth.' And you are interested in me, and in my problems – thank you!

PRAY

Bless, dear God, the work of Torch Trust. Help them to extend the reach of their ministries so that they can touch the lives of many more people with sight loss who are lonely, needy and feeling locked away from society. Amen.

ABOUT SUSAN POTTER

Susan worked for Torch Trust in various capacities for almost ten years from 1984. She remembers that her first task as a new staff member was to take part in an evening session at a houseparty for young people – something she found very daunting! Susan now lives and works in the Midlands and is an active member of a lively Baptist church.

OUTREACH

Torch Trust is both global ministry and personal touch.

There is a need for 'big picture' strategy when we look at our UK and international braille and audio production programmes; when we consider how to serve our network of Torch Fellowship Groups across the UK; when we plan our holidays to deliver the right mix of enjoyment, physical and spiritual refreshment for our blind and partially sighted guests.

But day by day we are reminded that our ministry is so often effective on the personal level. We have the privilege of talking and praying with individuals who phone our library lending service. We experience the joy of praying with someone on one of our holidays who decides to give their life to God. We see the gratitude on the face of a blind woman in a Malawian village when we give her a small sack of maize to feed her desperately poor family. We listen with gladness when the lonely blind person who sees hardly anyone day to day tells us how much his Torch Fellowship Group meeting means to him.

ENCOURAGEMENT

'Billy rather reluctantly volunteered to become a driver for the local fellowship group! Irene and Billy called for one dear old lady and brought her to the Torch Fellowship Group meeting. As she slowly manoeuvred her Zimmer frame along the passageway she said, "You don't know how much I look forward to coming to these meetings! It's my life! It's my treat of the month!" Billy thought about that. "Fancy it meaning all that to this old lady. I'll have to find out more about it." He started to go to church regularly with Irene and found the Lord himself!'

From **Coping with the Camel (1996)** *by Stella Heath*

'I have learnt to trust Jesus and to love and know Jesus more.'

Miss W *of* Bury, *a member of the Torch Library*

> God uses people. God uses people to perform His work. He does not send angels. Angels weep over it, but God does not use angels to accomplish His purposes. He uses burdened broken-hearted weeping men and women.

– David Wilkerson, pioneering evangelist among New York gangs in the 1960s

> It is the duty of every Christian to be Christ to his neighbour.

– German church reformer Martin Luther

MULTI-SENSORY FOCUS

How well do you manage your time? How do you remember things like appointments or birthdays and anniversaries? Do you make space in your week for spending time with people? Do you give time to church, social and community commitments? Is your life too full? Or too empty? How much time do you spend on your relationship with God?

For this next series of readings, have to hand your diary or appointments calendar and either a clock or a watch. These objects will be used to help you to think about your use of time as you pray.

THIS WEEK'S CONTRIBUTORS

JEFF BONSER • TREVOR ROACH • JAN DEAKIN • JONATHAN LAMB
LORIMER FINK • STEPHANIE SERGEANT • REV'D RICHARD BEWES OBE

OUTREACH: Unexpected meeting

Acts 8:29–33,35

The Spirit told Philip, 'Go to that chariot and stay near it.'

Then Philip ran up to the chariot and heard the man reading Isaiah the prophet. 'Do you understand what you are reading?' Philip asked.

'How can I,' he said, 'unless someone explains it to me?' So he invited Philip to come up and sit with him.

This is the passage of Scripture the eunuch was reading:
'He was led like a sheep to the slaughter....'

The eunuch asked Philip, 'Tell me, please, who is the prophet talking about, himself or someone else?' Then Philip began with that very passage of Scripture and told him the good news about Jesus.

Jeff Bonser writes

Picture the scene. I was at the national Christian Resources Exhibition, being held at Sandown Racecourse in Surrey. The entire New Testament was being read out loud. At the designated time, it was my turn and I went forward to read from wherever the previous person had left off. To my astonishment, the passage before me was the one I was due to lead at my home group that night – the story of Philip and the Ethiopian in Acts 8.

God was obviously saying something to me about telling the good news of Jesus. Unknown to me at the time, I went on to become the director of the Christian Enquiry Agency – an evangelistic outreach ministry to unchurched people. This passage has stayed with me ever since.

God guided Philip so clearly. How important it is to pray about the day ahead – asking God to use you with those you know you will meet and those you don't. Philip

> **Be ready to respond to the unexpected opportunities God has for you**

could have ignored the chariot – no doubt he'd got other places to go, people to see. Be ready to respond to the unexpected opportunities God has for you, and he promises to help.

Philip got involved with what the man was doing and then was asked about Jesus. In my experience, it doesn't often happen that way. But it's always good to take an interest in the people you come across. Be a good listener and, of course, be ready to say something about the difference Jesus makes in your life. No need to use 'religious' words; just tell it as it is. As it says in 1 Peter 3:15, 'Always be prepared to give an answer to everyone who asks you to give the reason for the hope that you have. But do this with gentleness and respect.' You could be the only Christian that person meets today.

PRAISE

Thank you, Lord, for the hundreds of people who work for Torch as volunteers, willing to share the story of their hope with people with sight loss all over the country.

REFLECT

Are you 'prepared to give an answer' today about the hope that you have? Look in your diary or on your calendar for times coming up in the next few weeks when you will be with people who don't know Jesus. Why not mark those days with the sign of a cross or in some other way to represent your willingness, with God's help, to share the reason for your hope with those people?

PRAY

Help me, Lord, to get involved with other people's lives, to be a good listener, and to earn the right to share about my own life with them. Amen.

ABOUT JEFF BONSER

Jeff Bonser is a trustee of Torch and has 25 years' experience in broadcasting and communications. He helped set up the commercial radio stations Essex Radio and Premier Christian Radio, and became the first director of the Churches Media Council. In 2001 Jeff was appointed director of the Christian Enquiry Agency where he developed national evangelistic outreach projects. He is now a deacon of Market Harborough Baptist Church and project manager of Sing Christmas, an evangelistic broadcasting initiative.

OUTREACH: Plenty of room

JOHN 14:1–6

Jesus said:

'Do not let your hearts be troubled. Trust in God; trust also in me.
My Father's house has plenty of room; if that were not so, would I have told you that I am going there to prepare a place for you? And if I go and prepare a place for you, I will come back and take you to be with me that you also may be where I am. You know the way to the place where I am going.'

Thomas said to him, 'Lord, we don't know where you are going, so how can we know the way?'

Jesus answered, 'I am the way and the truth and the life. No one comes to the Father except through me.'

TREVOR ROACH WRITES

I wrote this song, inspired by today's passage.

TEMPORARY HOME

This is my temporary home; I'm not going to be here forever.
This is my temporary home; I'm going to be with my Lord and Saviour.

No more sorrow and pain;
No more walking round in the rain;
No more looking over my shoulder;
No more seeing man's love grow colder.

This is my temporary home; I'm not going to be here forever.
This is my temporary home; I'm going to be with my Lord and Saviour.

Is this your temporary home; are you going to be here forever?
Is this your temporary home; are you going to be with your
Lord and Saviour?

No more sorrow and pain;
No more walking round in the rain;
No more looking over my shoulder;
No more seeing man's love grow colder.

What a joy to know that we can be safe and secure in the One who gave his life for us and be at peace with him.

> ...we can be safe and secure in the One who gave his life for us

REFLECT

Look at your diary or calendar. What is today's date? Check your clock or watch. What is the time?

One day clocks will stop and diaries will be redundant. Trevor asks us, 'Is this your temporary home? Are you going to be here forever?' If you know the security of God's promise of being with Jesus for all eternity, beyond the dimensions of earthly time, you can praise God. If you are at all unsure, you might like to pray the prayer you can find at the end of the book. If you can say this prayer from your heart and mean it, your future security is guaranteed.

PRAY

I pray for all the outreach opportunities you give to Torch – through the fellowship groups around the country, through the Torch Singers visits to churches, through contacts made by professional people working with blind people, through the radio programme Insight, through the magazines, through the lending library. Father, use all these means of outreach to help many understand how God loves them and wants to give them a secure future. Amen.

ABOUT TREVOR ROACH

Trevor's family is from Barbados. Trevor was born prematurely and he explains his sight loss as the result of too much oxygen at birth. Between the ages of five and 16, Trevor attended a boarding school for blind children. During his teenage years he struggled with everything from being bullied and hating schoolwork to racial prejudice. Trevor's talent for music helped pull him through this difficult period. He has a real gift for playing guitar, piano and drums. Trevor has known Torch since 1975 when he came to a young people's houseparty. He is currently employed in audio production.

OUTREACH: Without a shepherd

MATTHEW 9:35–38

Jesus went through all the towns and villages, teaching in their synagogues, proclaiming the good news of the kingdom and healing every disease and sickness. When he saw the crowds, he had compassion on them, because they were harassed and helpless, like sheep without a shepherd. Then he said to his disciples, 'The harvest is plentiful but the workers are few. Ask the Lord of the harvest, therefore, to send out workers into his harvest field.'

JAN DEAKIN WRITES

When Jesus saw the crowds, his heart went out to them in loving concern because, like sheep without a shepherd, they were unable to rescue themselves from the predicament they were in. In common with us, they thought, spoke and behaved in ways that displeased God and fell short of his holy standards.

Only Jesus could save them from God's condemnation and eternal punishment. Jesus loved us so much that he died on a cross to rescue us from this plight, taking on himself God's punishment for all our sins. Now everyone who believes in Jesus is forgiven, welcomed into God's family, and receives his gift of righteousness and eternal life.

Everyone needs to know what Jesus has done for them. I have to ask myself: does my heart go out in compassion to people who don't know Jesus? And am I making myself available to God to help make him known in whatever ways he shows me?

Jesus saw that there were many people to be reached and too few workers to complete the task, and he told his disciples to pray that God would send out more workers. So let's get on with it!

> **Everyone needs to know what Jesus has done for them**

REFLECT

Do you ever feel overwhelmed by the size of any task before you? When we think of the task of reaching a world of lost people with the Good News of Jesus Christ before he returns to judge the world, we may feel even more overwhelmed. However, nothing overwhelms Almighty God. Amazingly, he seeks our partnership in the task. He asks us to pray for more workers. Today, every time you check what the time is, will you pray that the Lord of the harvest will send out more workers into his harvest field?

PRAISE

I praise you, Lord, for all the events where Torch Trust is represented – from local meetings at clubs for blind people to national happenings such as Spring Harvest, Keswick, Sight Village and the Christian Resources Exhibition. May God's love for the lost be an essential part of the message communicated at all these events. Amen.

PRAY

Whether my diary is full or empty, Lord, help me not to forget my responsibility to share the love of Jesus in word and action to all those around me. Amen.

ABOUT JAN DEAKIN

Jan Deakin has been involved with Torch since becoming a Christian in 1973. She has been involved in two Torch Fellowship Groups, serving on the leadership team of one of them. She enjoys reading Torch magazines in braille and listening to books from the audio library. Jan is a member of Gunnersbury Baptist Church where she sings in the music group. She works with the Methodist Church as an administrator with particular responsibility for mission partners serving in other parts of the world.

OUTREACH: In word and life

1 Thessalonians 1:5

… because our gospel came to you not simply with words but also with power, with the Holy Spirit and deep conviction. You know how we lived among you for your sake.

Jonathan Lamb writes

Have you ever watched a news report on TV where the sound and vision are 'out of sync'? It's hard to take it seriously, as you try to match what is being said with the animated face on the screen. And it's the same in ordinary life: when someone's life fails to match their words, we give up listening.

Paul's description of the evangelistic task was not restricted to communicating information. He adds three other expressions: the gospel is proclaimed in God's power, with the Holy Spirit and with full conviction. But there is a further phrase that is closely connected to the rest of the verse. Paul says, 'you know how we lived among you for your sake.'

The gospel he proclaimed was also bearing fruit in his own life, and it was this combination that made gospel communication so effective. God's Word, proclaimed in the power of the Spirit, was embodied in the messenger himself. This is why Jeremiah called the prophets of his day to be consistent in word and life. 'They … live a lie,' he said (Jeremiah 23:14). They are not postmen who can live as they please as long as they deliver the mail. A prophet's life is part of his message.

Jesus was described as 'mighty in word and deed', for he proclaimed the truth and he embodied the truth. And we, his disciples, are called both to speak and to live the gospel. Authentic Christian evangelism is when word, Spirit and life combine together.

> ... we, his disciples, are called both to speak and to live the gospel

REFLECT

Looking at the clock, ask yourself: when are you at your best? Are you a morning or an evening person? Conversely, when are you at your worst? Take a moment now to consider what makes you 'out of sorts'. Is it tiredness, too many things to do, too many people, too few people? When is your life out of sync? Ask the Lord into all these areas so that the whole of your life may tell the same loving story.

PRAY

Please help those who take the lead in all areas of Torch work to be more like Jesus, showing compassion and concern for all. Inspire those who work with Torch Fellowship Groups; give them imaginative ideas to reach blind and partially sighted people within their localities. Amen.

ABOUT JONATHAN LAMB

Jonathan Lamb is known internationally as a Bible teacher and preacher. As a staff member of Langham Partnership International, he serves as Director of Langham Preaching, which seeks to encourage a new generation of Bible teachers around the world. Jonathan has served as chair of the Exeter Torch Fellowship, and is now a member of the Torch Council of Reference. He is also chair of the Keswick Convention, which is pleased to welcome a Torch group each summer.

OUTREACH: The plain truth

2 Corinthians 4:1,2

Therefore, since through God's mercy we have this ministry, we do not lose heart. Rather, we have renounced secret and shameful ways; we do not use deception, nor do we distort the word of God. On the contrary, by setting forth the truth plainly we commend ourselves to everyone's conscience in the sight of God.

Lorimer Fink writes

Have you ever lost heart when your witnessing for Jesus just hasn't worked out in the way you'd hoped? Telling others about God can be difficult. Introducing Jesus into the flow of a conversation can seem so very hard to achieve.

It is 'through God's mercy' that we ourselves know Christ and it is only through him that we have the desire and courage to even contemplate testifying about the good news that we have come to know.

Telling others doesn't need fancy words or awkward mini-sermons; it just needs the love of God within us and the love of God for others.

Sometimes it may be that just a few words introduced naturally into a conversation will be picked up by the person or persons listening. It may be that the conversation continues with no other obvious reference to spiritual things – but, still, you have done what the Spirit has prompted you to do. God will use whatever you say, no matter how apparently insignificant, to establish a foundation in someone's life on which the Spirit can work. One day the moment will come when 'the truth [can be set forth] plainly…' and, on that day, the full gospel of God's amazing salvation will come before that person – and you will have played a part in their journey.

So, take heart, be natural and God will open the way.

PRAISE

Thank you, Father God, for all those who have shared the gospel of Christ with me along the way. I praise you, too, for your life-changing Word, the Bible, which has spoken to my heart so often. And for all the good Christian books that have helped me grow.

REFLECT

Take your diary and, as you look back over recent weeks, think about how many meetings and conversations you've had with different people. Were there any opportunities to share the love of Christ that you missed? What would you have said if you had the chance again?

PRAY

Father, make me more aware of the possibilities of speaking up for Jesus – and help me to rely on the Holy Spirit to supply the words. Bless and make fruitful the ministry of Torch Trust, Lord, increasing opportunities to communicate the good news of Jesus and giving Holy Spirit freedom to share it with joy. Amen.

ABOUT LORIMER FINK

Having known Torch for many years, Lorimer describes it as 'a particular joy' to begin work as a librarian with the trust over seven years ago. She feels her involvement with Torch has deepened and grown as the work itself has grown. She is married to Mike, a teacher, and they have three grown daughters, two of whom are married. Lorimer and Mike are also enjoying being grandparents.

OUTREACH: Making friends

Matthew 28:18–20

Then Jesus came to them and said, 'All authority in heaven and on earth has been given to me. Therefore go and make disciples of all nations, baptising them in the name of the Father and of the Son and of the Holy Spirit, and teaching them to obey everything I have commanded you. And surely I am with you always, to the very end of the age.'

Stephanie Sergeant writes

God has given each of us the means to carry out these words from Matthew's Gospel. Just as the parts of a human body are all different, so each person in a local church has differing gifts and ministries. 1 Corinthians 12:18 says, '… in fact God has arranged the parts in the body, every one of them, just as he wanted them to be.' Our individual experiences make us uniquely fit to reach certain people with the gospel – and it is exciting to find who those people are.

I find my guide dog is an excellent evangelist! She is so good at making friends with people. I am often asked if she can be stroked, which gives me a really good opening for a conversation. One woman I met had had breast cancer, and she was taking her little boy to the children's hospital for treatment for leukaemia. My dog nosed around their seat on the train, hoping no doubt for crumbs from the pushchair. When I chatted to the woman, it became clear that she was angry with God about her situation. I gave her my phone number, and suggested she rang whenever she needed too. Twelve years later, she is a believer, and asks for prayer whenever she has a crisis.

Yesterday I was swimming alongside a woman who told me that her son was looking for redeployment within the company he works for. I offered to pray that he is given a job. Later I also prayed that he would find Jesus through this experience.

I long for all those I meet to find and know more of God. Whether it's colleagues at work, the operator at the phone call centre, or the milkman. Of course, I do get distracted sometimes. Someone once texted me a recipe for spicy meat balls, and I regret that I didn't manage to bring Jesus into that conversation! I find it's a good test of how close I am to God, as to whether I talk about him to people.

> **I long for all those I meet to find and know more of God**

I think evangelism starts, continues and finishes with prayer – and even if we lack opportunity we can pray.

REFLECT

Pick up your watch. When could you give some time to pray for people you know who are in need of God? Today? Do you long, like Stephanie, for people you meet to find God? If you have lost that longing, ask God to restore it, so that he can use you to pray for others and draw them to God. Could you encourage someone with a card, a phone call or an email?

PRAISE

I praise you, Lord God, for the hundreds of people who have heard about Jesus and come to faith through Torch activities in the UK and around the world.

PRAY

Give me love for others, dear Lord, as you love me. Amen.

ABOUT STEPHANIE SERGEANT

Stephanie and her guide dog Adele share their home with 24 friends, as she is a member of the Jesus Army! Stephanie trains blind people to use computers with assistive technology. She was born blind and, after schooling, went on to get a degree in psychology. She is a regular borrower of braille books from the Torch Library and also uses Torch's audio and tactile Christian resources to enable her to lead a cell group in her church.

OUTREACH: Set on fire

ACTS 8:29–35

The Spirit told Philip, 'Go to that chariot and stay near it.'

Then Philip ran up to the chariot and heard the man reading Isaiah the prophet. 'Do you understand what you are reading?' Philip asked.

'How can I,' he said, 'unless someone explains it to me?' So he invited Philip to come up and sit with him.

This is the passage of Scripture the eunuch was reading:
'He was led like a sheep to the slaughter…'

The eunuch asked Philip, 'Tell me, please, who is the prophet talking about, himself or someone else?' Then Philip began with that very passage of Scripture and told him the good news about Jesus.

RICHARD BEWES WRITES

How is the saving message of Jesus Christ most effectively spread? St Augustine gave the answer sixteen hundred years ago, when he explained, 'One loving spirit sets another on fire!' So it was, around the Roman empire of that first century AD. Christ was being shared one-to-one along 50,000 miles of Roman trunk road.

Luke gives us this superb example from a Greek believer, Philip. Though Philip was first noted for his administrative gifts, his desire to share Christ with others began to override all else, and many were touched by his witness.

One loving spirit sets another on fire!

Here, he is prompted by the Lord to intercept a single individual – a top official returning from a visit to Jerusalem in his chariot. The right place, the right person, the right book…

It was as well that Philip ran! In his reading, the traveller had got as far as Isaiah 53. It is all about the coming suffering Servant of the Lord – and that gave Philip his opening. The sins of us all, he explained, were laid on this unique Person in the death and judgement that he bore; this sacrifice of forgiving love originated in the mind and heart of God; and this world Saviour was none other than Jesus, once crucified – now alive for ever. Forgiveness was free! Philip's companion was won to Christ and baptised that very day.

'One loving spirit sets another on fire!' Something like 100,000 individuals are finding eternal salvation in Christ every day.

REFLECT

Look at your watch or clock. What time is breakfast for you? How about lunch and supper? Coffee breaks? If you're like most people, you rarely forget to eat! How reliable is your memory when it comes to prayer? Today, every time you check your watch to see if it's time for a meal, why not briefly pray for one person who doesn't yet know Jesus?

PRAISE

I rejoice with the angels, Father, over all those finding Jesus today! Thank you, Lord, for all the people who have become Christians through half a century of ministry of Torch Trust.

PRAY

Fill me, Father, with your Spirit, so that I may be on fire for you. Amen.

ABOUT RICHARD BEWES

Richard Bewes, a son of missionaries and raised in Kenya, was formerly Rector of All Souls Church, Langham Place. These days he maintains his ministry on a wide front – recent travels having taken him to Africa, Europe, Asia and the USA – as he works with a number of Christian agencies in the UK and overseas. Richard also hosts various international on-screen Bible discussion programmes, and has written over 20 books. He received the OBE in 2005 for services to the Church of England.

WEEK 3

SPIRITUAL HUNGER

Just as physical hunger is a normal sign of a healthy body, so spiritual hunger is a normal sign of a healthy spirit. We need to feed on the Bible and on good Christian literature to nourish our souls and help us grow as Christians. Access to spiritual food is not as easy for people with sight loss as for those who are sighted. The whole Bible in braille, for example, takes up almost two metres (six feet) of shelf space; and on audio it would fill many CDs. But for those who want to read the Scriptures in accessible formats, Torch makes them available at an affordable cost or on loan.

As well as the Bible, Torch Trust now offers 3,000 Christian books in a range of accessible formats in its library – the largest Christian library for blind people in the UK. About a dozen new titles are added every month. The range available includes theological, devotional, missionary, biographical and Christian leisure reading. Torch Trust also produces a range of regular magazine publications, daily Bible readings, and hymn and song books for people with sight loss.

ENCOURAGEMENT

'… there will be no braille in heaven … but let us use our braille … to the utmost so that the family of God in heaven is complete.'

From Coping with the Camel (1996) *by Stella Heath*

'Your Giant Print books let me read slowly, stop and think. They remind me that God never leaves me alone and isolated, I can turn to my Torch Library books to keep me going.'

Mrs P *of London*

> **The enjoyment of [God] is the only happiness with which our souls can be satisfied... Fathers and mothers, husbands, wives, or children, or the company of earthly friends are but shadows, but enjoyment of God is the substance. These are but scattered beams, but God is the sun. These are but streams, but God is the fountain. These are but drops, but God is the ocean.**
>
> *– Jonathan Edwards, eighteenth century American theologian*

'It's wonderful to be able to borrow part of the braille Bible relevant to our house group, enabling me to fully participate.'

Mr R *of Crowborough*

'Thank you for the Scripture Union Daily Bread daily notes which I find so helpful and understandable. I do appreciate them, so easy to listen to.'

Mrs E *of Basingstoke*

MULTI-SENSORY FOCUS

Jesus said, 'I am the bread of life. He who comes to me will never go hungry, and he who believes in me will never be thirsty' (John 6:35). Jesus is all that is needed to sustain us in our spirits. This week have available a slice of bread whenever you take time to pray and read God's Word. Jesus called himself the 'bread of life' and bread serves as a reminder of the central role of Jesus in giving us life, health and strength. Have you been feeding on him regularly? Or have you been starving your spirit?

THIS WEEK'S CONTRIBUTORS

TIM MALAIDZA • THE VEN. RICHARD ATKINSON • REV'D MARGARET CUNDIFF
EILEEN COLE • CAROL EDDON • JAN TURNER • JEFF LUCAS

SPIRITUAL HUNGER: Satisfied

MATTHEW 5:6

Blessed are those who hunger and thirst for righteousness,
for they will be filled.

TIM MALAIDZA WRITES

The human body needs food to keep it alive and strong. We need to eat good, nourishing food at the right time and every day to satisfy our physical hunger. As Christians we don't just depend on physical hunger, but we have a spiritual hunger that craves to be satisfied. Our spiritual hunger is often neglected because we become satisfied with the material things that meet only our physical hunger. Jesus warns us of the danger in Luke 12:15 where he says, 'life does not consist in an abundance of possessions.'

> Our spiritual hunger is often neglected because we become satisfied with the material things that meet only our physical hunger

For spiritual hunger to be satisfied, there needs to be a mind set on it. We read in Matthew how Jesus was led by the Holy Spirit into the wilderness to fast. After Jesus fasted for forty days, Satan tempted him to feed his physical hunger, but he answered Satan that 'Man shall not live by bread alone, but by every word of God' (Luke 4:4 KJV). Jesus also told us that we are blessed if we hunger and thirst after righteousness, for we shall be filled.

Are you hungry for more of God today? This hunger can only be satisfied by reading the Word of God regularly; fellowshipping with other Christians and spending time talking to and listening to God through prayer.

REFLECT

Look at your slice of bread. If you ate that now, how long would it be before you became hungry again? And what would you do about it? Probably you would feel hungry in just a few hours; and most of us have the means to go to the kitchen and find more food quite easily. Think about how much you enjoy a meal when you are really hungry. But have you ever asked God to show you your spiritual poverty and to make you really hungry for him? We can echo Tim's prayer of gratitude that God never runs out of food to meet our deepest spiritual hunger.

ABOUT TIM MALAIDZA

Tim worked as the Director of Education for the Blind in Malawi for 20 years. During this period his Christian faith encouraged him to look for the spiritual well-being of the blind students as well as pursuing education for them. When Torch Trust was established in Malawi he was appointed the first Secretary of the Council. When he retired from government, he worked as Torch administrator for seven years; he continues today as honorary treasurer.

SPIRITUAL HUNGER: Open table

LUKE 7:36–39,50

When one of the Pharisees invited Jesus to have dinner with him, he went to the Pharisee's house and reclined at the table. A woman in that town who lived a sinful life learned that Jesus was eating at the Pharisee's house, so she came there with an alabaster jar of perfume. As she stood behind him at his feet weeping, she began to wet his feet with her tears. Then she wiped them with her hair, kissed them and poured perfume on them.

When the Pharisee who had invited him saw this, he said to himself, 'If this man were a prophet, he would know who is touching him and what kind of woman she is – that she is a sinner.'

… Jesus said to the woman, 'Your faith has saved you; go in peace.'

RICHARD ATKINSON WRITES

Who is hungry in this vivid event from our Lord's life? At first sight it is the Pharisee – named in verse 40 as Simon – who is about to sit down and eat. In reality it is the woman, for she is hungry for the love of Jesus.

Simon, the man of religion, should have known spiritual hunger but he is blind to the living Word present before him; he 'doesn't appreciate God's generous love when it sits in person at his own table' as theologian Tom Wright says in his commentary *Luke for Everyone*. In contrast the woman who lives a sinful life, who flouts social convention by letting down her hair and who embarrasses everyone as she wipes and kisses Jesus' feet, is desperately hungry;

> **Jesus' table is open to anyone who is spiritually hungry**

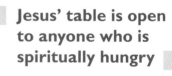

she knows the truth of her condition; she knows she needs forgiveness and healing; she needs to be fed.

Jesus' table is open to anyone who is spiritually hungry. Many years ago when I was a vicar in Sheffield I opened the vicarage door to Richard, a man I knew to be a drug dealer. He simply said, 'I want to change my life.' Within a few days he was with a Benedictine community who shared with him the love of Christ.

George Herbert's wonderful poem 'Love bade me welcome' speaks of Christ's invitation to all who are spiritually hungry. It challenges us not to draw back but instead ends with the promise of being fed: 'You must sit down, says Love, and taste my meat: So I did sit and eat.'

REFLECT

Pick up your piece of bread. You cannot taste it simply by holding it; you must take a bite and chew it to experience its flavour. It won't benefit your body unless it becomes a part of you. It's the same with God's Word. Today, as you chew over this wonderful story, try to imagine yourself in that setting with Jesus. Who would you be: Simon the Pharisee or the woman with the perfume? As you become part of the story and the story becomes a part of you, how do you feel?

PRAISE

Thank you, Father God, that your table is open to all.

PRAY

We pray for all who feel lonely, isolated or socially excluded because of sight loss. May they experience the warm welcome of being invited to your table. Use Torch Trust to draw many into friendship with Jesus and his family. Amen.

ABOUT RICHARD ATKINSON

Richard is currently Archdeacon of Leicester with responsibility for the Church of England in the city and the east of the county. He is a member of the Torch Trust Council of Reference. Before coming to Leicestershire, he served in the Sheffield Diocese for 15 years. His committed community involvement led to him being awarded an OBE for service to the unemployed in Rotherham. He is married to Helen, a Professor of Engineering at Leicester University, and has three teenage children.

SPIRITUAL HUNGER: Miracle

JOHN 6:25–29,35

When they found him on the other side of the lake, they asked him, 'Rabbi, when did you get here?'

Jesus answered, 'Very truly I tell you, you are looking for me, not because you saw the signs I performed but because you ate the loaves and had your fill. Do not work for food that spoils, but for food that endures to eternal life, which the Son of Man will give you. On him God the Father has placed his seal of approval.'

Then they asked him, 'What must we do to do the works God requires?'

Jesus answered, 'The work of God is this: to believe in the one he has sent.'

… Then Jesus declared, 'I am the bread of life. Whoever comes to me will never go hungry, and whoever believes in me will never be thirsty.'

MARGARET CUNDIFF WRITES

The crowd followed Jesus because they had heard about and seen the amazing things he had done. They listened intently to his words. Could this be the one promised by God who would come and save them? On and on they followed him, wanting more. The miles and time meant nothing. But then tiredness and hunger overtook them, and there they were: stranded, unable to go any further.

Then the miracle happened. Seemingly out of nowhere Jesus provided a meal for them – enough and more for everybody. If he could do that, then all their worries were over! Nothing was beyond his power, so why not make him their king and he would give them everything they wanted?

But it was what we call 'cupboard love.' They wanted him for what they could get out of him, failing to recognise the grace and power of God. Jesus was offering them himself, the bread of life. They just wanted ordinary bread.

What do you long for most of all in your life today? Is it physical and material security? Is it someone to take responsibility for the problems and demands in your life which cause you so much anxiety? That would be wonderful, wouldn't it? Or are you hungry and thirsty for the living God, to know the inward strength and peace only he can give? The good news is that Jesus offers that to us right now. I can ask, 'Bread of heaven, bread of heaven, feed me now and ever more' – and praise him that he does!

> **... are you hungry and thirsty for the living God, to know the inward strength and peace only he can give?**

PRAISE

Father God, thank you so much that you give us 'food that endures to eternal life.' Forgive us for seeking our satisfaction in wrong places and wrong ways.

REFLECT

Feel the texture of your bread. If you have been using the same slice of bread all week, by now it is probably already going dry and spoiling. As you hold onto the bread, hold on in your heart to the thought that what Jesus offers you will never go dry and spoil; you can draw strength from it at any time; it is always fresh and new.

PRAY

Lord, please bless the work of the transcription team at Torch House and of the many volunteer transcribers who work from home. Help them to produce many titles in braille, giant print and audio media which feed the hunger of people's souls. Amen.

ABOUT MARGARET CUNDIFF

Margaret is an Associate Minister of St James Church in Selby, North Yorkshire, where she has lived since 1970. She is an author and broadcaster, and writes a weekly column for the Selby Times. She has recorded a number of her books for Torch, something she regards as a special privilege. Margaret is also chaplain at York Minster and at the Yorkshire Air Museum. She is married to Peter and they have two grown children.

SPIRITUAL HUNGER: Maturity

1 Peter 1:23 – 2:3

For you have been born again, not of perishable seed, but of imperishable, through the living and enduring word of God. For,

'All people are like grass,
and all their glory is like the flowers of the field;
the grass withers and the flowers fall,
but the word of the Lord endures forever.'

And this is the word that was preached to you.

Therefore, rid yourselves of all malice and all deceit, hypocrisy, envy, and slander of every kind. Like newborn babies, crave pure spiritual milk, so that by it you may grow up in your salvation, now that you have tasted that the Lord is good.

Eileen Cole writes

When I was a small baby, my mother had a problem. She wanted to breast feed me but, after a few minutes of vigorous sucking, I would open my mouth and yell indignantly! She did not have enough milk. It was no use offering me a dummy or a thumb to suck; I was still hungry and I would scream as loudly as I could until I was given a bottle!

God has provided food for our souls in the Bible, which Peter calls 'pure spiritual milk'. But are we feeding on it?

As babies grow, they need to be weaned onto solid food and are given hard crusts to encourage them to chew. As we read the Bible, we will find some parts that are easy to understand while others are more complicated! It can be tempting to give up struggling with a difficult passage and go back to the parts we know and love – just like a baby that spits out solid food and wants milk all the time! The author of the letter to the Hebrews knew people like that: 'You need milk, not solid food! Anyone who lives on milk, being still an infant, is not acquainted with the teaching about righteousness. But solid food is for the mature, who by constant use have trained themselves to distinguish good from evil' (Hebrews 5:12–14).

So, even if we cannot always understand all we read, let us persevere; and God will help us grow into mature Christians.

> **God has provided food for our souls … But are we feeding on it?**

REFLECT

How hard is the crust on your slice of bread? It's the crust that takes the most chewing! We often cut the crusts off for young children – but as we grow older we may find that it's the most enjoyable part of the bread! The next time you come to a 'difficult' part of scripture, take time to chew it a bit longer. Ask the Holy Spirit to help you understand – perhaps by sending you someone to explain it or through a commentary or by some other illustration – so that you grow into a more mature Christian.

PRAISE

Thank you, Lord, for the wisdom and insight we gain from all those who write daily Bible reading notes; and for Torch's partnerships with those like CWR, SU and BRF who publish them.

PRAY

We ask you to bless and inspire all Christians who write to bless and encourage others – whether that's in church magazines, devotional publications or other Christian books; and bless those who write for Torch magazines. May the words they use to support and nourish their readers be yours. Amen.

ABOUT EILEEN COLE

Eileen was born into a Christian family and gave her heart to Jesus at an early age. Having learned braille with the idea of becoming a home teacher for those with sight loss, she heard about Torch and eventually began writing out books for the braille library. In 1973 she went to Hurstpierpoint, joined the Torch staff and spent over 20 years working in the library there and later at Torch House in Hallaton before her retirement.

SPIRITUAL HUNGER: Complete

JOHN 10:7–11

Therefore Jesus said again, 'Very truly I tell you, I am the gate for the sheep. All who have come before me are thieves and robbers, but the sheep have not listened to them. I am the gate; whoever enters through me will be saved. They will come in and go out, and find pasture. The thief comes only to steal and kill and destroy; I have come that they may have life, and have it to the full.

'I am the good shepherd. The good shepherd lays down his life for the sheep.''

CAROL EDDON WRITES

Jesus is the only one who can satisfy all our longings – and when we seek him we can know him as the shepherd who takes care of all our needs.

I am sure you will have noticed how often people resist responsibility. They will try to 'pass the buck'. 'That's not my job,' they will say. Or 'you'll have to speak to someone else about that.'

> Jesus is ... so willing and able to take full responsibility when I come to him with my spiritual hunger

One of the reasons I love Jesus is that he's so willing and able to take full responsibility when I come to him with my spiritual hunger. He'll never turn me away – nor will he turn you away. Just as the eastern shepherd was totally committed to supplying all that was needed for the wellbeing of the flock in his care, so Jesus has undertaken to give protection, security, satisfaction – everything needed and much more besides! – to everyone who believes and trusts in him. Jesus has opened the way for us to enjoy life in the way it was originally intended that we should enjoy it. Through Jesus, we can enter in to God's family and know deep joy and fulfilment.

We know that the eastern shepherd went to extreme lengths for his precious sheep. At night he lay down to become the gateway to the sheep enclosure, protecting them with his own body against the predators who were likely to be prowling around ready to attack these vulnerable creatures. In the same way, Jesus gave everything he could possibly give to rescue us from the powers of evil when he died for us on the cross.

Jesus wants the very best for each child of God. His amazing love makes our lives complete.

PRAISE

Lord, we rejoice that so many people with sight loss in contact with Torch Trust – many hundreds of them around the world – have entered into the joy of salvation and the security of knowing Jesus as their Great Shepherd.

REFLECT

Take your piece of bread and tear it into pieces as you think about how the body of Jesus was broken. This, though, was no destructive act – but the fulfilment of long-awaited promises for a Saviour who would rescue his people from the eternal consequences of sin. Because of the death of Jesus, we can know reconciliation with God and experience the joy of knowing we will one day be united with him in heaven.

PRAY

Father, so many people are living empty lives devoid of purpose and robbed of fulfilment. Give us compassion to pray for them and to share the good news of Jesus with them whenever we can. Amen.

ABOUT CAROL EDDON

Carol gave her life to Jesus at the age of 21, after studying the Bible for herself at home. Two years on, she became involved in the work of Torch and joined the staff in 1972. Ten years later, she moved to Bristol to marry Peter, who is now safe in God's keeping. Carol continues to work as a volunteer braille proofreader and is a Torch trustee.

SPIRITUAL HUNGER: Seeking

Matthew 6:31–33

So do not worry, saying, 'What shall we eat?' or 'What shall we drink?' or 'What shall we wear?' For the pagans run after all these things, and your heavenly Father knows that you need them. But seek first his kingdom and his righteousness, and all these things will be given to you as well.

Jan Turner writes

Abraham Maslow, the renowned psychologist, asserts that there are five levels of human need related to fulfilling our identity and purpose: physiological (the very basics for life such as water, food, shelter); safety (personal and financial security, and good health); social (support of friends and family); self esteem; and self-actualisation (realising one's potential).

The Bible shows that we all have a deep spiritual need which can only be satisfied by knowing the Lord Jesus. We are designed to be in fellowship with God our Father, and we can only do this through his Son Jesus Christ. By understanding God's teaching through the help of the Holy Spirit, we can be led through faith into his eternal kingdom.

If you have not put your trust in the Lord, then you will be dissatisfied. That hunger may show in the longing for other things such as power, money, fame or material security. Left to our own devices, we will all hunger for the wrong things.

What are you hungering for today? If you recognise that there is a spiritual emptiness in your life that needs filling by the love of God, you can start to draw close to him by admitting that you fall very

> **If you have not put your trust in the Lord, then you will be dissatisfied**

short of God's standard of perfection. You can know deep within you that Jesus Christ has paid the price of sinfulness for each one of us so that we can have an eternal relationship with him. Perhaps you know the truth of all this, but recently you have begun to hunger after the wrong things. You can return to God in a second! For true satisfaction and purpose in life we need to follow the command of Jesus: 'Seek first his kingdom and his righteousness…' (Matthew 6:33)

PRAISE

Father, I thank you so much for promising to meet all my needs. I need your grace to help me to see where I am spiritually poor and to invite you to make me the person you would want me to be.

REFLECT

Look at the broken pieces of bread. As you think about each area of need, pick up one piece to represent that need, asking God to meet that need in your daily experience. Think about your basic physical needs such as food and a home; your need for a secure place to live in and enough to live adequately; your social needs; your emotional wellbeing; your need to fulfill your potential. Finally, think about your spiritual needs. God is able to bless you in all these areas.

PRAY

So often it is blind and partially sighted people who are the least well resourced and supported in our communities. Lord, bless the work of Torch Trust so that many more people with sight loss can have their deepest needs met in you. Amen.

ABOUT JAN TURNER

Jan has been blind from birth and for 23 years she had an additional disability that confined her to a wheelchair. Though still blind, on Boxing Day 2007 she experienced a miraculous healing from God which enabled her literally to jump for joy. Jan has been a reader of Torch literature since her teens and became a Christian through working alongside Torch co-founder Stella Heath.

SPIRITUAL HUNGER: Empty

PSALM 42:2–5

My soul thirsts for God, for the living God.
    When can I go and meet with God?

My tears have been my food
        day and night,
        while people say to me all day long,
        'Where is your God?'

These things I remember
        as I pour out my soul:
        how I used to go to the house of God
        under the protection of the Mighty One
        with shouts of joy and praise
        among the festive throng.

Why, my soul, are you downcast?
        Why so disturbed within me?
        Put your hope in God,
        for I will yet praise him,
        my Saviour and my God.

JEFF LUCAS WRITES

It was a rainy afternoon and, forsaking the possibility of an overpriced Starbucks, I decided to take a few quiet moments in the incense-perfumed quietness of Westminster Cathedral. There I met one of the most spiritually hungry men of my lifetime. He was riding a motorised wheelchair, his shattered body lay almost flat. Toggling his chair around to face the altar, he stared at the crucifix, a broken man facing a broken man. And then, with huge effort that was evidently painful, he lifted a mangled arm in a salute; costly worship from someone who urgently felt his need of Jesus. Like the psalmist, like a hungry man with a hollow stomach, or a Sahara traveller tormented by thirst, my unknown friend with the salute was doing everything he could to connect with and honour the Lord Jesus.

Christianity makes a terrible hobby. The Bible is filled with people so desperate for Jesus that they interrupt his meals, shout at him in the streets and wreck his planned days off. Perhaps you feel your need of Jesus very urgently. Once again you are smeared with failure, disappointed by your own inconsistency, taunted by what you feel is a lack of faith. But your hunger for change, for holiness, and for God himself is the sweetest worship; with Jesus, those who feel themselves filled are sent away empty, while those who feel their emptiness and impoverishment are welcomed and accepted.

> **... your hunger for change, for holiness, and for God himself is the sweetest worship**

REFLECT

Do you remember being told not to talk when your mouth's full? Well today, imagine your mouth is full with your bread. Don't talk! Instead, take a few minutes to listen. We often spend our prayer time talking to God. That's good, of course – but we need to listen too. Linger over the words in today's reading. Read them several times. What are they saying to you? What is God saying to you through them?

PRAISE

Thank you, Lord, that there is no need in my life that you are unable to meet.

PRAY

Father, give wisdom to everyone in leadership in Torch Trust. Give them trust as they recognise that the work is yours; and give them faith to believe that you are fully able to resource the work completely. Amen.

ABOUT JEFF LUCAS

Bible teacher Jeff Lucas travels internationally with a specific vision to encourage and equip the Church. He is part of the leadership team of Spring Harvest, and the author of 14 books as well as a number of study guides, booklets and a DVD teaching series called 'Life Journeys'. He is an ambassador for Compassion, an international charity working to help children in poverty. Jeff and Kay live in Loveland, Colorado, where he holds a teaching post at Timberline Church, Fort Collins.

WEEK 4

FELLOWSHIP

Sight loss frequently leads to isolation and loneliness. Torch Trust has long recognised the social needs of blind and partially sighted people. Around 120 Torch Fellowship Groups meet around the UK, most getting together on a monthly basis for varied programmes. Many people find the group is a real lifeline.

ENCOURAGEMENT

'I returned from my first visit to Torch House in Sussex in an excited state. I had been one of the guests at a weekend houseparty, and I had been given an introduction to Torch's outreach work through Christian literature in audio, braille and large print. I was filled with admiration of all I'd witnessed.

'Yet… there was something still needed, something even more personal. What could it be?

'And as I prayed and thought, the conviction grew strongly upon me that the answer was to augment this vital outreach by person to person involvement. This was the vision given, the seed sown in my heart to provide some means of meeting together on a regular basis – hence the forming of the first Torch Fellowship Group in the home of Barbara Cudmore in Birmingham where I was then living.

'This was January 1970. Who can now calculate the blessing in and through the Fellowship Groups in those years and indeed in future years – till the Lord comes!'

Blind pianist Peter Jackson

'What I hope Torch never gives up on is … the commitment to interdependence – with blind and sighted people together – each serving the other.'

Christine

'The meetings are such a good way to come to know Jesus, and they give me courage.'

Miss E of Edinburgh

'In all the time I've gone to the TFG, I've always felt accepted. It gives focus to my month too.'

Miss L of Edinburgh

'When I moved here, worried about how I would settle, the most amazing thing happened. In a queue in a shop, I met someone from the local Torch Fellowship Group. I knew it must be God leading me.'

Franek

'My first impression of a TFG meeting was a warm feeling of love in the place and everyone helping everyone!'

Miss J of Edinburgh

Our love to God is measured by our everyday fellowship with others and the love it displays.

– Theologian, preacher and author Andrew Murray

MULTI-SENSORY FOCUS

'There are few hours in life more agreeable than the hour dedicated to the ceremony known as afternoon tea,' said author Henry James. So often in our communities, a cup of tea or coffee symbolises the intimacy of friendship. As you spend time with God in reading and prayer this week, have your favourite mug or cup beside you to help you explore the theme of fellowship.

THIS WEEK'S CONTRIBUTORS

REV'D DR DEREK TIDBALL • IAIN LACKIE • JENNIFER REES-LARCOMBE
REBECCA COLPUS • DAVID PALMER • ANDRÉ CLOWES • LAPSON MBEWE

FELLOWSHIP: Companionship

1 Corinthians 1:9; Romans 6:5

God is faithful, who has called you into fellowship with his Son, Jesus Christ our Lord.

... If we have been united with him in a death like his, we will certainly also be united with him in a resurrection like his.

Derek Tidball writes

Fellowship is more than sharing a cup of tea and a biscuit, although that's often what we mean by the word. To the Christian it is a grand word. The greatest privilege of all is not that we have fellowship with each other but with Jesus Christ. That's at the heart of the Christian's calling.

> ... spending time with Jesus means we become like him

Fellowship means companionship. Like Enoch, who 'walked faithfully with God' (Genesis 5:24), we are called to live our days in company with Jesus. What a difference it makes to remember that he's always at our side! Spending a lot of time in a friend's presence means you become like them. So, spending time with Jesus means we become like him.

This friendship grows as we do ordinary things throughout the day but, as with any companionship, it grows stronger if we devote quality time to talking together. So we need to listen to his words and chat to him in prayer.

Fellowship is more than this. It means participation. So, to have fellowship with Jesus is to join with him in death to sin and resurrection to life. In Brazil, when men drink tea they don't drink from their own cups, but share the pot by drinking through a common straw and passing it round the circle. That's true fellowship and illustrates how united we should be with Christ.

REFLECT

What form does your prayer usually take? How do you invite the Lord into your circumstances?

When you have a cup of tea with a friend or companion, you don't have to think about what to say. You just converse with each other quite naturally. Sometimes it's simply about the weather; other times it's something deeper. If you were sharing a cup of tea with Jesus right now, what would you talk to him about? What do you think he'd say to you?

PRAISE

We praise you, Lord, for the joy of spending time with you and with each other. How blessed we are to know this fellowship! Thank you for being our caring companion as we journey through life.

PRAY

Glorify Jesus through the work of Torch Fellowship Groups, as they seek to draw into fellowship many blind people who live alone and feel forgotten. Amen.

ABOUT DEREK TIDBALL

Derek Tidball is a Baptist minister who was Principal of the London School of Theology (formerly London Bible College) for 12 years. Author of about 20 books, he now lives in Leicester and devotes his time to writing, speaking and supervising postgraduate studies. He is a member of the Council of Reference of Torch Trust.

FELLOWSHIP: Forgiven

1 JOHN 1:7

But if we walk in the light, as he is in the light, we have fellowship with one another, and the blood of Jesus, his Son, purifies us from all sin.

IAIN LACKIE WRITES

The first time the word 'fellowship' significantly impinged on my consciousness was when, in a certain church in Edinburgh, it used to be announced that we would have 'fellowship in a cup of tea after the service.' I used to think that this must be a particularly large cup to accommodate all those present in the church at the time! I soon came to discover that 'fellowship' is one of those words which can quickly become devalued into merely having a little chat with someone, with or without the cup of tea thrown in!

There are two elements which make this 'fellowship' about which the apostle John speaks truly Christian.

First, we are people who know Jesus Christ. I remember this becoming very clear to me when, in a Baptist church in Rijeka in Croatia, I met a lady with whom I only had a few words of bad French in common. However, despite the language difficulty, we were able to share together the great truth that we knew the same Saviour.

> **... we are the fellowship of the forgiven**

Secondly, we are the fellowship of the forgiven; our sins have been dealt with by the shedding of the blood of Christ. Whether it is in a Torch meeting, preaching in my own church or in general conversation, to speak of this is always the greatest of joys.

May our fellowship be always dependent on the truth that we know Jesus and the forgiveness that he gives. My prayer is that he will help us in all we say and do to share these great joys with others.

PRAISE

I praise you, Lord, for the unity that I am able to have with other Christians because of the shared joy of knowing Jesus and his forgiveness.

REFLECT

Who do you like to have a cup of tea with? Perhaps you could invite someone to tea who doesn't yet know the joys of Christian fellowship? Each time you pour yourself a drink today, think of one person you could invite for tea. Pray for them and for the opportunity to share the gospel with them.

PRAY

Give compassion and understanding to all who organise and volunteer at Torch Fellowship Groups. May their work be really effective in creating genuinely close bonds of fellowship among people with sight loss in their locality. Amen.

ABOUT IAIN LACKIE

Iain went to the Royal Blind School in Edinburgh and from there to Edinburgh University to study history. He became a Christian in 1972 and later went on to a career in computing. He has been receiving Torch literature since 1972 and has been the regional co-ordinator of Torch work in Scotland since 2001. His interests include books, music and cricket; and he is a fan of the long-running Radio 4 soap, *The Archers!*

FELLOWSHIP: Connectedness

1 JOHN 1:2,3

The life appeared; we have seen it and testify to it, and we proclaim to you the eternal life, which was with the Father and has appeared to us. We proclaim to you what we have seen and heard, so that you also may have fellowship with us. And our fellowship is with the Father and with his Son, Jesus Christ.

JENNIFER REES-LARCOMBE WRITES

I used to hate the word 'fellowship.' As a teenager, to me it meant having to go into the church hall after the service to drink tepid tea while everyone else talked – but never me! If that was 'fellowship' I certainly didn't want it!

> **Fellowship isn't tepid tea; nor is it a sentimental feeling**

Now, of course, I've come to realise that fellowship means infinitely more than that. It was used by the first Christians to describe the way they loved one another and shared their homes and possessions: 'They devoted themselves … to fellowship, to the breaking of bread and to prayer … All the believers were together and had everything in common' (Acts 2: 42,44). They felt closer than a family because Jesus, by his Holy Spirit, was living in each of them, which also united them with one another. 'Fellowship' is a word that describes this kind of deep connectedness.

When a doctor in ancient times wanted to describe conjoined or Siamese twins who had only one heart and shared the same blood, he would say they shared 'fellowship of blood.' In other words they were as closely connected as it is possible for human beings to be.

Jesus was connected to his Father so closely, and his desire was that we should be joined in the same way to our fellow believers: 'As the Father has loved me, so have I loved you … Love each other as I have loved you' (John 15:9,12).

Jesus must feel so sad when he sees the way Christians ignore or even fall out with one another, when he wants us to be really close. Perhaps you respond, 'But some Christians are impossible to love!' Well, if it feels impossible to *feel* love for some people; with God's help it is never impossible to *show* love! Fellowship isn't tepid tea; nor is it a sentimental feeling. It is the loving way we act and react to our fellow Christians.

PRAISE

I praise you, Lord, for all the acts of kindness I see from believers which promote true fellowship.

REFLECT

Have you heard the phrase, 'to get a handle on something', meaning to find a way of coping with a difficult problem? We all know at least one person who irritates or annoys us. Take your cup or mug by the handle as you ask God to show you how to 'get a handle' on loving them.

PRAY

Father God, may Torch Fellowship Groups be increasingly more accessible and inclusive of unchurched people and not-yet-Christians. Through friendship over cups of tea, we ask that the greatest joy of fellowship – a shared belonging to Jesus – can be known. Amen.

ABOUT JENNIFER REES-LARCOMBE

Jennifer Rees Larcombe is a counsellor who runs a Christian organisation called Beauty from Ashes, aiming to help people through loss, grief and trauma of all kinds. When her six children were small, a virus made her a wheelchair user for eight years. She was miraculously healed through prayer in 1990. She has 13 grandchildren and lives in the country with two dogs – Stella who is blind and Phoebe who is deaf.

FELLOWSHIP: God's family

LUKE 8:1–3

After this, Jesus travelled about from one town and village to another, proclaiming the good news of the kingdom of God. The Twelve were with him, and also some women who had been cured of evil spirits and diseases: Mary (called Magdalene) from whom seven demons had come out; Joanna the wife of Chuza, the manager of Herod's household; Susanna; and many others. These women were helping to support them out of their own means.

REBECCA COLPUS WRITES

We all need friends around us. Even Jesus appreciated this. Having chosen twelve men to be his closest friends, he was also supported by a group of women. These women came from a range of backgrounds and they stayed with Jesus all the way to the cross and were with him when he died. They also arranged for the rituals for Jesus' burial. We also read of them after the resurrection meeting with the apostles and other believers for fellowship and prayer, and they were present when the Holy Spirit came at Pentecost.

Do we sometimes feel that we have to live our Christian lives on our own? There are times when our friends do not seem to be there for us. Jesus had to face times like that too. At the cross, when he needed support the most, many were too afraid to stand by him. But the women remained faithful. They could say or do little for Jesus, but they were with him.

> ... let us remember the model Jesus gave us – to live as a member of God's family

In our materialistic world where the rights of the individual are valued more highly than a sense of community, let us remember the model Jesus gave us – to live as a member of God's family, supporting and being supported by our Christian brothers and sisters, sharing God's love and reaching out to the lonely.

REFLECT

Taking your cup or mug in your hand, run a finger round the rim in a clockwise direction, tracing a complete circle. Now think about the circles you move in: family, friends, church, work, other social groups. Where do you get support? Give thanks for each circle of contact. Now run your finger in the opposite direction and ask yourself: Who do I give support to? Give thanks for these people too.

PRAISE

Lord, I thank you for the circles of contact Torch has with blind associations and groups working with disabled people. May this support be mutual; and may Torch have opportunities to share its Christian ethos to a wider world through these contacts.

PRAY

Father, help me to bless my circles of contact by sharing the love of Jesus. Amen.

ABOUT REBECCA COLPUS

Born in the south of England, Rebecca now lives in Westmoreland. She is keenly committed to promoting and selling Traidcraft goods. She also has a career in the charity sector, including experience in the Citizens Advice Bureau and Age Concern. She has worked for Torch as a Regional Networker.

FELLOWSHIP: Community

ACTS 2:42–47

They devoted themselves to the apostles' teaching and to fellowship, to the breaking of bread and to prayer. Everyone was filled with awe at the many wonders and signs performed by the apostles. All the believers were together and had everything in common. They sold property and possessions to give to anyone who had need. Every day they continued to meet together in the temple courts. They broke bread in their homes and ate together with glad and sincere hearts, praising God and enjoying the favour of all the people. And the Lord added to their number daily those who were being saved.

DAVID PALMER WRITES

In 1979 the American pop group of four sisters called 'Sister Sledge' launched a record entitled 'We are family'. It's a great thought! As Christians, we're all part of a family – some closer than others.

> **We can celebrate God's generosity by being generous ourselves**

These verses from Acts give us a snapshot of early church life. Note how frequently we see terms like 'they', 'all', 'together' and 'their'. There is a deep sense of belonging, fellowship and sharing, undergirded by a love for God and a commitment to each other.

It's a highly attractive picture of a truly loving Christian community, in spite of the problems we read about which developed later. It's also a huge challenge to us in our Western churches – often consumer-minded, fragmented and individualistic. However, when Christians start to model the behaviour of the Acts community, they often find a new spring in their step. Suddenly there is an attractiveness and energy about life when people stop clinging onto everything and start sharing with others. We can celebrate God's generosity by being generous ourselves.

When I worked with a small church in the slums of Lima in Peru, I discovered that while materially they had little, yet spiritually they were incredibly rich. Commitment to God and people characterised the growing church. It was magnificent to witness!

In our often unattractive, stagnant or humdrum churches we need to ask: What's not happening that needs to happen? The gospel hasn't changed. People still need rescuing. We are God's family. So what are we doing to strengthen family ties?

PRAISE

Lord, we thank you for all the new Torch Fellowship Groups that have started around the country. We ask that they may know the joy of loving fellowship together.

REFLECT

Is your cup an old favourite? Or brand new? To a lot of people a cup is just a cup! But maybe yours is special because of its history? Or because it was a gift? As you hold it, think about someone you care about who needs to know Jesus or who needs God to answer some specific need in their life. Ask our generous God to bless them. You could even buy them a new mug as a sign of your love!

PRAY

Lord, help me to experience the loving community that you want me to enjoy, even if that means learning to be less selfish and materialistic. Amen.

ABOUT DAVID PALMER

Canadian by birth, his working life has been hugely varied – ranging from being a buyer for a major wine company to running his own market garden. In 1992 he met Marie from Belgium on a train and they later married. They have a lively 12-year-old, Simon. David currently works with Torch Trust as Regional Outreach Leader, overseeing the network of Torch Fellowship Groups around the UK. As part of his brief, he also seeks to help churches be more welcoming and accessible for people with sight loss.

FELLOWSHIP: Friendly aid

ACTS 2:32–35,42,44

God has raised this Jesus to life, and we are all witnesses of the fact. Exalted to the right hand of God, he has received from the Father the promised Holy Spirit and has poured out what you now see and hear. For David did not ascend to heaven, and yet he said,

'The Lord said to my Lord:
"Sit at my right hand
until I make your enemies
a footstool for your feet".'

… They devoted themselves to the apostles' teaching and to fellowship, to the breaking of bread and to prayer.

… All the believers were together and had everything in common.

ANDRÉ CLOWES WRITES

I have very strong memories of the primary school I attended during the war. In particular, I remember that the morning assemblies always included reciting the Apostles' Creed. From this creed comes the phrase: 'I believe in the communion of saints…' It didn't make much sense to me then but now, as I re-assess the phrase, I find myself asking: What does it mean?

As I was thinking of this, I came across the verse of an old hymn of Charles Wesley:

> Help us to help each other, Lord,
> Each other's cross to bear;
> Let each his friendly aid afford
> And feel his brother's care.

'That's it!' I thought, 'That's what it means!'

It doesn't simply mean that Christians belong to a particular group or community, though that may be true. Rather, it's about caring, about sharing, about partnership, about involvement never forced but always genuine and spontaneous. One word describes this in the New Testament – the word 'fellowship'.

Many are familiar with the words from the church marriage ceremony: 'for better, for worse, for richer, for poorer, in sickness and in health, to love and to cherish…' That's what fellowship is all about: personal responsibility for each other.

Welcome to the communion of saints, and to all that it means!

> **… it's about caring, about sharing, about partnership, about involvement never forced but always genuine and spontaneous**

REFLECT

How many cups and mugs do you own? How many do you need? If you have a large family or lots of friends, you need lots of cups. But how many cups don't get used? What could you do with them so that someone benefits from them? Take them to a charity shop perhaps? Or sell them at a car boot sale and give the money to the homeless? What else do you have lots of that you don't use? Is there some small way in which you could follow in the footsteps of the first church?

PRAISE

Thank you, Lord, for the community of saints who are helpers, drivers, befrienders, speakers and tea makers at the monthly Torch Fellowship Group meetings around the country.

PRAY

*Help us to help each other, Lord,
Each other's cross to bear;
Let each his friendly aid afford
And feel his brother's care.
Amen.*

ABOUT ANDRÉ CLOWES

André was born in the Staffordshire moorland town of Leek. During the Second World War, the family moved to live in Stoke-on-Trent. He became a Christian at Sheffield University. After graduating and qualifying as an architect he met and married Audrey. Moving to Leicester in 1973, André became aware of the work of Torch Trust and supported it with much interest, eventually being invited to join the board of trustees on which he served for a number of years until 2008.

FELLOWSHIP: All for Jesus

JOHN 3:22,23,25–30

After this, Jesus and his disciples went out into the Judean countryside, where he spent some time with them, and baptised. Now John also was baptising … An argument developed between some of John's disciples and a certain Jew over the matter of ceremonial washing. They came to John and said to him, 'Rabbi, that man who was with you on the other side of the Jordan – the one you testified about – look, he is baptising, and everyone is going to him.'

To this John replied, 'A person can receive only what is given from heaven. You yourselves can testify that I said, "I am not the Messiah but am sent ahead of him." The bride belongs to the bridegroom. The friend who attends the bridegroom waits and listens for him, and is full of joy when he hears the bridegroom's voice. That joy is mine, and it is now complete. He must become greater; I must become less.'

LAPSON MBEWE WRITES

'Our village has been visited by the Lord.'

We were so challenged to hear from Nkhundi that we were the first people to visit them with the gospel message. The village is in a typical mountain bush area with good soil for farming. Many people came to hear what we had to say.

We went there to preach the Word of God in response to the spiritual hunger of the people. The response after the preaching was wonderful and many were moved and challenged.

Not only were spiritual needs met but we were able to consider people as a whole and think about their physical needs. We wanted people to see the open hands of the Lord. When Jesus went around preaching the Word, he did not only preach but he also helped the poor and healed the sick. So, after the church service, people were given some practical help. We distributed clothes, soap and medicine to those who were sick.

After a week, the village chief sent a message to me saying that his village had been changed by our visit – and he saw our visit as the Lord's. 'Many people in my village are talking of the love of God, which took you from your village to visit us. The village, which used to be quiet, is now noisy due to the happiness of the people,' he said.

> **... we are seeking that when people look at us they should see the Lord**

In all that we do, we are seeking that when people look at us they should see the Lord. This is what John's message in this Bible passage is all about. None of this is for us; it is all for Jesus alone. As John says, 'He must become greater; I must become less.'

REFLECT

Fill your cup or mug with water, tea or coffee. When the mug is empty, the mug is all-important. When the mug is full, what is inside is more important. Are you an empty mug, full of your own importance? Or are you so full of Jesus, that he is more important?

PRAISE

We thank you, Father, for all those who take leadership in Torch Trust in whatever way – in administration and stewarding finance, in organising fellowship groups, and in communicating the good news of Jesus to blind and partially sighted people.

PRAY

Lord, may all I do bring glory to you and be for the growing of your kingdom. Amen.

ABOUT LAPSON MBEWE

Lapson is an African pastor. He has a heart for blind and partially sighted people and spends a lot of time visiting and encouraging them. He has planted churches in Malawi and Mozambique. Lapson is married to Ellen and they have three children. In addition, Lapson and Ellen care for over 100 orphaned children and 22 widows.

WEEK 5

REST AND RENEWAL

'Come to me, all you who are weary and burdened, and I will give you rest,' is the invitation of Jesus (Matthew 11:28). The Christian experience is characterised by the deep peace that we can find in knowing Jesus, together with the energising refreshment of new beginnings.

Often we have a need to step aside from the routine of life for a time of rest and renewal. There are particular challenges for those with sight loss in trying to take a holiday. Torch Trust runs holidays with a strong family ethos, most of them based at the Torch Holiday & Retreat Centre in Sussex and others at carefully-chosen venues around the UK.

ENCOURAGEMENT

'Hospitality [at Torch Holiday & Retreat Centre] is second to none. It has lifted us up spiritually and physically. We have booked to come again twice this year.'

Holiday guest Ms M from Northamptonshire

'I am so thrilled to have found something worthwhile to do and now have a purpose for living.'

Torch volunteer Mr M from Gloucester

'My holiday was like a feast that lasts forever. It gave me a taste of things to come in heaven. I had 24-hour Christian love and care.'

Holiday guest Ms J from Nottinghamshire

Every now and then go away, have a little relaxation, for when you come back to your work your judgement will be surer. Go some distance away because then the work appears smaller and more of it can be taken in at a glance and a lack of harmony and proportion is more readily seen.

– Leonardo Da Vinci, Italian painter, sculptor and scientist

'Fabulous food … made lots of new friends. A truly blessed time! All the staff and volunteers were wonderful, ready to meet our every need.'

Holiday guest Ms A from South Wales

'The Lord has revitalised my spiritual and physical life.'

Holiday guest Mrs L of Faringdon

MULTI-SENSORY FOCUS

An unnamed writer has given us this lovely thought: 'Today is a smooth white seashell; hold it close and listen to the beauty of the hours.' This week, it would help your reflection and prayer if you have a shell at hand. If you don't have a shell you could choose to have nearby one or two other things that remind you of holiday times – a pebble or piece of rock, a fir cone, a souvenir from a favourite place, your passport or bus pass, even a bottle of sunscreen!

THIS WEEK'S CONTRIBUTORS

REV'D ROY SEARLE • SUSAN MOORE MBE • DR SUSAN HAMMOND
DR MIKE TOWNSEND • JOYCE OWENS • PETER JACKSON • GAIL MILLAR

REST AND RENEWAL: Sabbath

GENESIS 2:1–3

Thus the heavens and the earth were completed in all their vast array.

By the seventh day God had finished the work he had been doing; so on the seventh day he rested from all his work. Then God blessed the seventh day and made it holy, because on it he rested from all the work of creating that he had done.

ROY SEARLE WRITES

'Thank God for the Sabbath wherein all things gain their true perspective,' wrote William Wilberforce.

> **Sabbath ... is about freedom and life**

The Scriptures remind us of the gift of sabbath. While 'sabbath' can mean a single day, its principle is revolutionary for the whole of life. It is a radical means of maintaining life and is a building block of a healthy society. Sabbath affords us rest. It should not be viewed in a legalistic way, which Jesus condemned. It is about freedom and life, not prohibition and judgement. Sabbath is, however, important. It represents the importance of play and recreation as a counterpart to work. It reminds us that being busy is not necessarily a virtue but can mean avoidance of those things in life that are essential for our wellbeing, namely relationships – with God, self and others. Busyness can also rob us of one of God's greatest gifts: the gift of rest.

Sabbath reminds us that we are called not so much to be consumers, which is a grotesque description of humanity made in the image of God, but that we are called to be persons in relationship, those who commune.

Observing the Sabbath requires discipline. For example, it may involve learning to *be* and not to be always *doing*, playing with the kids rather than being on the computer, going for a walk in the country or city rather than shopping, pottering rather than getting that project completed, spending time with neighbours and friends.

For fast acting relief on bland predictability and weariness, observe the sabbath; rest, recuperate and be renewed. Remember the sabbath and live!

REFLECT

Pick up your shell or fir cone and, as you hold it, imagine yourself in your favourite kind of holiday place. Are you beside the sea, listening to the sound of the waves gently breaking on the beach? Strolling by a lakeside listening to the sounds of children laughing in the paddle boats? Sitting on a picnic bench in a wooded country park with the occasional sound of birdsong? Even thinking of taking a break can be refreshing! Daydream about how and where you like to relax, and thank God for opportunities for rest.

PRAISE

I give you thanks, Lord, for the Torch Holiday & Retreat Centre. Thank you for the relaxed family atmosphere which enables people who are blind and partially sighted to enjoy a Sabbath rest.

PRAY

Help me, Father, to achieve a good balance of work and rest in my life. Amen.

ABOUT ROY SEARLE

Roy Searle lives with his wife Shirley in Northumberland; they have four children and two grandchildren. Roy came to faith while an Outward Bound Instructor. He is a founder leader of the Northumbria Community and a former President of the Baptist Union of Great Britain. He is a popular writer and speaker on issues of spirituality and mission, leadership and culture. He has given valuable consultancy to Torch Trust on issues of transition and is a member of Torch's Council of Reference.

REST AND RENEWAL: At his feet

LUKE 10:38–42

As Jesus and his disciples were on their way, he came to a village where a woman named Martha opened her home to him. She had a sister called Mary, who sat at the Lord's feet listening to what he said. But Martha was distracted by all the preparations that had to be made. She came to him and asked, 'Lord, don't you care that my sister has left me to do the work by myself? Tell her to help me!'

'Martha, Martha,' the Lord answered, 'you are worried and upset about many things, but few things are needed – or indeed only one. Mary has chosen what is better, and it will not be taken away from her.'

SUSAN MOORE WRITES

When thinking about rest, my thoughts turn to this very real and human situation of Jesus' visit to Martha and Mary. It is understandable that Martha felt she had been left to do everything. I often try and imagine the scene of Mary sitting at Jesus' feet, listening to his every word. She obviously felt there was nothing so important, even in the midst of a very busy day.

Many of us live in ways where every minute of our days seem to be accounted for. We rush from one meeting to another; we eat hurried meals. Then there are church activities, sometimes taking up several evenings a week. Some mothers of young children have

> **Fixing my eyes on Jesus has become my greatest desire over the years**

to work full time. Parents are stretched as they juggle with all the demands on their time and energy.

I wonder if sometimes we feel that Jesus is excluded from our daily and sometimes frantic activities? Fixing my eyes on Jesus has become my greatest desire over the years. It's wonderful to spend time in his presence, trying to take in his amazing, forgiving love for me.

PRAISE

Thank you, Father God, for the many opportunities Torch Trust is able to give to people with sight loss to travel to new places. Please bless all those who are going on Torch's regional holidays this year to lovely venues across the UK.

REFLECT

Think about these dictionary definitions of 'holiday': a day on which work is suspended; a day free from work that one may spend at leisure; a day on which custom or law dictates a halting of general business activity to commemorate or celebrate a particular event. But Susan says that, for her, rest and renewal is about sitting at the feet of Jesus. Pick up your holiday reminder items and think about your own definition of holiday. Is Jesus part of that definition?

PRAY

Lord, true rest and renewal are found in knowing you. Whatever my plans for holiday times this year, help me to remember that. Amen.

ABOUT SUSAN MOORE

Susan spent 18 months working in the Torch Library and office, a time she recalls as 'extremely happy' and she adds, 'Reading many of the Christian books in braille helped my faith more than I can say.' Since then Susan has worked in London, including periods at the Methodist Church Overseas Division, various banks and four education authorities. Susan currently works for the Qualifications & Curriculum Authority. She still uses Torch literature today. She was awarded the MBE for services to education and the visually impaired.

REST AND RENEWAL: Creation

PSALM 121:1–4,7,8

I lift up my eyes to the mountains –
    where does my help come from?
My help comes from the LORD,
    the Maker of heaven and earth.
He will not let your foot slip –
    he who watches over you will not slumber;
indeed, he who watches over Israel
    will neither slumber nor sleep.

… The LORD will keep you from all harm –
    he will watch over your life;
the LORD will watch over your coming and going
    both now and forevermore.

SUSAN HAMMOND WRITES

Isn't it fantastic that the Lord is always there for us! He constantly watches over us and keeps us from harm, now and forever. What an assurance! Yet so many of us struggle through life, forgetting his promises, not listening to him. Often we're just 'too busy' to make time for God. 'I've got so much work to do…' Sound like you? Our lives can be so hectic that it seems impossible to take time out for God. Yet we all need to. We're constantly being told by health professionals to slow down and take some 'me time'. I suggest we'd do even better to have some 'God time'. But how?

> **Rest in God while the rain beats on the window…**

Here, the psalmist suggests that God can be found in the mountains.

Through his creation we can enjoy his presence and know that he is always there. Creation is everywhere so you *can* stop and be with him anytime, anywhere. Why not enjoy the tranquility of your garden or a park? Smell the flowers, listen to the birds, feel the wind on your face. Rest in God while the rain beats on the window, marvel at the clouds scudding across the sky, watch lambs frolicking in a field. If you're the adventurous type, like me, climb a mountain and feel the rocks beneath your feet. The list is endless. And know this: when you make time for God, he will restore your soul.

PRAISE

Thank you, Lord, for the beauty of all that you have created for us to enjoy. Help me to be aware of your creation as a gift from you, and to praise you for the opportunities it gives for rest and renewal.

REFLECT

As you hold your shell or cone, think about its shape, its beauty. Is it smooth or rough? Imagine the natural setting where it lay before it came into your possession. Using your senses, what parts of God's creation are you aware of today? Remember: you are the best part of God's creation and he takes delight in you.

PRAY

Father, I pray for all with sight loss who feel that taking a holiday is beyond their means or too difficult to manage. May many more of them learn about Torch Holidays and be enabled to take part in them. Amen.

ABOUT SUSAN HAMMOND

Susan thoroughly enjoys creation. A keen hiker and cyclist, she can often be found in the Lake District enjoying the peace that comes with being surrounded by God's beautiful garden. At other times, Susan often has her nose in a book or enjoys spending time with friends. She has worked at Torch House but is currently studying part time and hoping to qualify in counselling, so that she can be more effective in sharing God's love with others.

REST AND RENEWAL: Fragrance

JOHN 12:1–3

Six days before the Passover, Jesus came to Bethany, where Lazarus lived, whom Jesus had raised from the dead. Here a dinner was given in Jesus' honour. Martha served, while Lazarus was among those reclining at the table with him. Then Mary took about a pint of pure nard, an expensive perfume; she poured it on Jesus' feet and wiped his feet with her hair. And the house was filled with the fragrance of the perfume.

MIKE TOWNSEND WRITES

I love gardens. Not to garden but to relax in. There are some wonderful sensory gardens for blind people.

I love perfume. As I write, my garden is filled with the fragrance of orange blossom. I used to lodge with someone who had 250 rosebushes in his garden. One night I came home after a hard day's work and relaxed in his garden. I detected one particularly powerful fragrance.

'Mr Clark,' I said, 'what is the fragrance I can smell?' He laughed, 'There are thousands of roses here! But, come with me.' As we wound our way through the garden, the fragrance grew stronger. 'Here we are, Mike. Smell this.' The fragrance almost overwhelmed me. This was the special rose. 'What is this rose which out-fragrances all other roses?' I asked. 'Fragrant Cloud,' I was told.

The house at Bethany was filled with fragrance. It came from Jesus. Mary poured expensive perfumed ointment over Jesus' feet. Jesus'

> **Jesus longs to live through us, sharing his unique fragrant beauty with those around us**

beautiful fragrance was enjoyed by all except (as you'll see later in the Bible passage) Judas the thief.

Sadly, we all fail. Failure spoils our lives and can get between us and God. Jesus longs to live through us, sharing his unique fragrant beauty with those around us. Like the family at Bethany, we need to invite Jesus to share our busy lives. Why not spend some time today in a garden? Enjoy its beauty and fragrance. Meditate on the beauty of Jesus. Let his fragrance restore your spirits and permeate your surroundings.

PRAISE

Lord God, you have blessed me with many times of rest and relaxation and I thank you for them. May my words and my life be so sweetened by the fragrance of Jesus that the blessing is communicated to others.

REFLECT

Does your shell smell of the seashore? Does your pine cone carry the fragrance of the forest? Does your sunscreen carry an aroma of beach holidays? What smells can you recall from your last holiday? The fragrance of beautiful flowers? The exhaust fumes on the airport tarmac? The smell of onions from the hot dog stand? Thank God for memories of good times. And ask him what it would mean for your life to spread the fragrance of Jesus.

PRAY

Lord Jesus, may many blind people come to know you as Saviour, so that any empty stretches of their lives can be filled with meaning and they can experience true rest in you. Amen.

ABOUT MIKE TOWNSEND

Mike Townsend's links to Torch Trust go back as far as 1966, and currently he serves as both trustee and Technical Director. He is married to Edith and they have a daughter, Christine. Guide dog Tom is an important part of the family! Mike is a leader of Fleckney Baptist Church. He also serves as a trustee board member of both RNIB and Guide Dogs for the Blind. He travels internationally with these responsibilities and also as a Bible teacher and a trainer of trainers.

REST AND RENEWAL: Surrender

JEREMIAH 18:1–6

This is the word that came to Jeremiah from the LORD: 'Go down to the potter's house, and there I will give you my message.' So I went down to the potter's house, and I saw him working at the wheel. But the pot he was shaping from the clay was marred in his hands; so the potter formed it into another pot, shaping it as seemed best to him.

Then the word of the LORD came to me. He said, 'Can I not do with you, house of Israel, as this potter does?' declares the LORD. 'Like clay in the hand of the potter, so are you in my hand, house of Israel.'

JOYCE OWENS WRITES

The sudden onset of blindness meant the end of my nursing career and all hopes of going to the mission field. This was a bitter disappointment and I said to God, 'Of what use can I be for you now? Please show me the way forward.'

Finding myself in a rehabilitation centre where I had to attend pottery lessons was not the way I would have chosen. I felt rebellious, feeling that there was nothing useful I could do with my lump of clay.

But as I entered the pottery, the Lord spoke to me through the words of Jeremiah 18:6: 'As the clay is in the potter's hands, so are ye in my hands.'

Those words written on the wall were just for me. God was telling me that as the resting clay had to be placed in the hands of an experienced potter to be made into something beautiful, so did I have to surrender all to the divine potter to allow him to make me fit for his use. Only then

> **I have to surrender all to the divine potter to allow him to make me fit for his use**

did I find peace and lasting joy in his service, becoming sure that I was where God wanted me to be.

In the words of an old hymn by Joseph Parker:

God holds the key of all unknown,
And I am glad;
If other hands should hold the key,
Or if he trusted it to me,
I might be sad.

REFLECT

Take your shell or other holiday reminder object into your hands and feel its shape. Think about how the shape has been designed for a purpose or because of its natural setting. The shell has been shaped perfectly to house a small sea creature; the pebble has been worn smooth by the waves; the fir cone has been weathered by the wind. Even the bottle of sunscreen has been designed to suit the contents and to appeal to buyers. How has God shaped your life over the time that you have known him? Can you 'feel' how he has shaped you for his purposes?

ABOUT JOYCE OWENS

Reading a copy of a braille magazine, Joyce became aware of the work of Ron and Stella Heath, co-founders of Torch Trust. In the editorial Stella had written, 'It is not enough to know about God, you must know him personally and intimately if you are to know the true meaning of prayer.' Joyce's testimony is that during her many contacts with Torch over 48 years including attending many houseparties, she has found those words to be 'so true'.

REST AND RENEWAL: Nestling

MATTHEW 11:28–30

Jesus said:

'Come to me, all you who are weary and burdened, and I will give you rest. Take my yoke upon you and learn from me, for I am gentle and humble in heart, and you will find rest for your souls. For my yoke is easy and my burden is light.'

PETER JACKSON WRITES

There are four aspects to this lovely invitation given by the Lord Jesus.

'**Come**' This invitation is granted to us by no less than the Son of God. He knows all about weariness, about what it feels like to be crushed; and these feelings qualify us for the invitation with its attendant gift of rest.

'**take**' The yoke is not something that Jesus imposes upon us: we have to take, or humbly accept it. The yoke will keep us close to him, preventing our straying from his side. And it reminds us that we are fellow-workers with him in the life we live here on earth.

'**learn**' Some teachers can be authoritarian, bombastic and dogmatic. But Jesus, the teacher of all teachers, is 'gentle and humble in heart'. He is easy to live with, easy to learn from. There is so much to learn from him, and the 'L' plate will never

> In our coming to Jesus, working with him, and learning from him, we shall find the deepest, most satisfying rest imaginable: soul rest

fall from us until we are changed into his likeness, when he receives us to glory.

'find' In our coming to Jesus, working with him, and learning from him, we shall find the deepest, most satisfying rest imaginable: soul rest. Corrie Ten Boom once told an over-anxious man not to wrestle, but to nestle!

As a kind of postscript, Jesus adds: 'For my yoke is easy, and my burden is light.' He will never ask too much of us. The yoke and the work are made just for us.

PRAISE

I praise you, Lord God, because you never ask more from me than I am able to give; but you give to me with a generosity that is boundless.

REFLECT

Take your shell or fir cone and hold it in the palm of your hand. Is it heavy or light? Does what Jesus has called you to feel heavy or light? If it feels heavy, ask your Father to show you why that is. Do you need to trust more? Do you need to ask for the empowering of the Holy Spirit? Are you 'wrestling' rather than 'nestling'?

PRAY

Father God, I pray for all those in a position of responsibility and leadership in Torch Trust, that they may know the lightness of your yoke. Amen.

ABOUT PETER JACKSON

Peter lost his sight as a result of measles at the age of 18 months. He was taught to read and write braille and introduced to the piano. His ambition was to be a jazz pianist and he began playing at working men's clubs. Studying music and piano-tuning at college, he underwent a spiritual crisis and became a committed Christian. During a gospel mission in Guernsey, Peter met Margaret and they married in 1961. They have three children. Peter records music and travels extensively, speaking in churches, clubs, schools and prisons. He is the author of two books about his life, two songbooks and a book of poems.

REST AND RENEWAL: Energised

Matthew 11:28–30

Jesus said:

'Come to me, all you who are weary and burdened, and I will give you rest. Take my yoke upon you and learn from me, for I am gentle and humble in heart, and you will find rest for your souls. For my yoke is easy and my burden is light.'

Gail Millar writes

We all need rest. When God created the earth he gave us one day out of the seven for rest. How many of us use that day to rest from the busyness of our week? Or is it a day where we are even more busy?

Recently I completed a discipleship course called 'Lifeshapes' and in that I learned that God intends us to work from rest and not rest from work. How much more energised and clear-minded we are when we return to work or the routine of life having had a few days' rest. The Bible refers so many times to the need for rest and the benefits of rest.

In leading Torch Holidays, one of my greatest joys is seeing the consequences of enabling and encouraging people to rest. They are given time to unwind, to relax, to laugh, to be loved and cared for, to chat with others, to enjoy the countryside and to listen to God. As a result, their whole demeanour and personality changes over the course of a few days. It never ceases to fill me with joy to see the difference a few days can make to someone who

> In a place of rest we are all able to receive from God more clearly...

arrives tired, weary, worn down and finding everyday life a grind. Our holidays are not just about providing shelter or lodgings, we want to 'be Jesus' to all our guests – to give strength to the weary; to give encouragement, love, support, care and compassion; to share joy, peace, patience and kindness with them.

In a place of rest, we are all able to receive from God more clearly, as we give him time to speak and ourselves time to listen.

PRAISE

Thank you, Father God, for all the staff and volunteers who make Torch Holidays such an enriching experience for so many people with sight loss.

REFLECT

We started this week of readings with the quotation: 'Today is a smooth white seashell; hold it close and listen to the beauty of the hours.' Has reflecting on rest and relaxation enabled you to 'listen to the beauty of the hours'? As you put your shell or holiday reminder back in its usual place, make a resolution to build godly rest into both the routine of your life and into the special times of relaxation.

PRAY

Lord, there are so many blind people who need a break from the routine of life when they can be cared for and strengthened in a loving Christian environment. I ask that more resources will be made available to help that happen. Amen.

ABOUT GAIL MILLAR

Gail is the tireless and energetic leader of Torch Holidays, based at the Torch Holiday and Retreat Centre in Hurstpierpoint near Brighton. She previously worked as a catering manager for a hotel chain. She has been running holidays for people with sight loss for over 12 years. Gail is married to Stuart and they have five children – two married, two still living at home and one away studying – and one grandchild. Gail also serves on the leadership of a local church.

ALL GOD'S CHILDREN

The international outreach of Torch Trust is a vital arm of its ministry. Right from the beginning, Torch magazines have been sent to many readers overseas. But visits to three African countries in 1989 – made in response to God's prompting – launched a new and important phase.

'I felt ashamed of the materialism in our lives, and the casual way in which we treat God's goodness and provision for our needs. Those neat little Bibles we carry to church… telephones that work… constant water and power… good medical services… they are so much part of our western life that we hardly spare them a thought, except perhaps to grumble if they are not perfect!'

These were the thoughts of Stella Heath, Torch Trust co-founder, on her return from the five-week trip with colleague and former missionary Rosina Sharp.

Torch Trust has a braille production centre and base in Blantyre, Malawi, from which staff and volunteers can reach out to those with sight loss in Africa.

Over the years, Torch has also ministered to blind people in places such as Romania and Spain. Today Torch literature is sent out to 100 countries.

ENCOURAGEMENT

'When I trusted Jesus Christ by reading one of your magazines I felt wonderful, like a cow in a field of cassava!' (Nigeria)

'Your magazines have changed my life.' (Kenya)

'Your cassettes have brought me life.' (Malawi)

'I've been brought closer to God.' (Uganda)

'I now have an understanding of the spiritual life.' (Malawi)

'I couldn't live without my braille Bible volumes.' (Malawi)

'My spiritual life is always uplifted by your books. The Lord usually uses these stories to meet the present point of my need.' (Nigeria)

'I am totally dependent on Torch Trust. I am like a sheep and you are my shepherd.' (Malaysia)

> **The way from God to a human heart is through a human heart.**
>
> *– author Samuel Gordon*

> **The greatest thing a man can do for his Heavenly Father is to be kind to some of his other children.**
>
> *– Scottish writer Henry Drummond*

MULTI-SENSORY FOCUS

This week as you read and pray, it would be helpful to listen to the sounds of people from around the world. Do you, for example, have a favourite audio recording of world music – instrumental, orchestral, pop group or choir? Or do you have a short wave radio you could tune to a station from another country? If you have internet access, you could hear music or conversation in another language that way. Play your recording or radio at a low volume as an aid to thinking about people in other places around the world.

THIS WEEK'S CONTRIBUTORS

JESSICA WADE • REV'D DAVID COFFEY OBE • MICHELE GUINNESS • RONA GIBB
CURTIS LEE HALL • WINSTON CHIDZAMBUYO • JANET STAFFORD

ALL GOD'S CHILDREN: Fearless

1 Samuel 17:33,34,37,40,45,46

Saul replied, 'You are not able to go out against this Philistine and fight him; you are little more than a boy, and he has been a warrior from his youth.'

But David said to Saul ... 'The LORD who rescued me from the paw of the lion and the paw of the bear will rescue me from the hand of this Philistine.'

...Then he took his staff in his hand, chose five smooth stones from the stream, put them in the pouch of his shepherd's bag and, with his sling in his hand, approached the Philistine.

...David said to the Philistine, 'You come against me with sword and spear and javelin, but I come against you in the name of the LORD Almighty, the God of the armies of Israel, whom you have defied. This day the LORD will deliver you into my hands ... and the whole world will know that there is a God in Israel.'

JESSICA, WHO IS BLIND AND AGED 12, WRITES

My favourite Bible story is David and Goliath. Nobody thought David was going to win, including me! I was so surprised the first time I heard it. David had God and it made him bigger than Goliath. It made you that size; big enough to beat any Goliath.

JESSICA'S MUM WRITES

When Jessica was six years old she had to have a transplant. During this operation, she had a heart attack and nearly died. Then she was in and out of the operating theatre several times. Each time she was very afraid. Each time we would go and find our 'secret hiding place'

– a quiet little corner in the hospital, away from people. There we would quietly sing 'How sweet the name of Jesus sounds in a believer's ear'. And every time Jessica's fear evaporated.

How sweet the name of Jesus sounds in a believer's ear!
It soothes his sorrows, heals his wounds and drives away his fear.

David had God and it made him bigger than Goliath

REFLECT

Just like little Jessica, around the world people of every sort and condition are calling on God to soothe their sorrows, heal their wounds and drive away fear. Gently play your recording of voices or sounds from a different part of the world. Imagine all those voices, those spoken out loud and those silently expressed, calling on the name of Jesus. How wonderful that God can hear and understand everyone's cry – and he can hear yours!

PRAISE

Thank you, Father, that I am one of your children and that you hear the cry of my heart.

PRAY

Lord Jesus, I pray especially for blind and partially sighted people in countries with little access to Christian literature or other support that could ease their struggles. Be close to them. Use organisations like Torch Trust to reach out to them with the good news of the gospel. Amen.

ABOUT JESSICA WADE

Jessica was born blind and with several medical conditions. She lives in the London area, and enjoys school. She loves reading braille books from the Torch Library, especially biographies. Jessica is also a great football fan. Her favourite team is Manchester United and her favourite player is Wayne Rooney. Another of her enthusiasms is drama. At school she plays piano and drums. She would like to be a doctor one day and travel the world.

ALL GOD'S CHILDREN: Countless

GENESIS 22:17,18; REVELATION 7:9,10

'I will surely bless you and make your descendants as numerous as the stars in the sky and as the sand on the seashore. Your descendants will take possession of the cities of their enemies, and through your offspring all nations on earth will be blessed, because you have obeyed me.'

… After this I looked, and there before me was a great multitude that no one could count, from every nation, tribe, people and language, standing before the throne and in front of the Lamb. They were wearing white robes and were holding palm branches in their hands. And they cried out in a loud voice:

> 'Salvation belongs to our God,
> who sits on the throne,
> and to the Lamb.'

DAVID COFFEY WRITES

These two readings combine to make one of God's greatest promises in scripture. The promise is made to Abraham that his family would be as countless as the stars in the sky and the sand on the seashore. It took great faith to believe this promise when Abraham and his wife were old people who had been in a childless marriage for many years. But this is why Abraham and Sarah are commended for their faith: because they believed that God would do what he had promised.

In time their miracle baby Isaac was born and the promise of God's large family begins to unfold through the story of salvation in the Old Testament.

The promise begins a new chapter on the Day of Pentecost when the Church goes international and

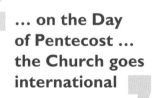

… on the Day of Pentecost … the Church goes international

God-fearing Jews from numerous nations become some of the first converts to the early Church.

By the time we reach John's vision in the last book of the Bible we see the ultimate fulfilment of the promise made to Abraham. The countless number of God's family promised to Abraham is now standing before the throne of God with their songs of endless praise and thanksgiving.

This is God's global family at worship. I'm so glad that from the beginning of the world God planned a world family of different people with different voices who could unite in their praise and worship of Jesus Christ.

PRAISE

How glad I am, Father, that one day countless believers from every corner of the globe will be together at your throne, praising you! Thank you for saving me to be one of that number.

REFLECT

As you listen to your world music quietly playing, imagine that amazing scene described in Revelation, with an international multitude singing the praises of God. Can you see your own face in the crowd?

PRAY

I pray for the Torch work based at the braille production centre in Malawi. Lord, I ask that through Torch Trust many people with sight loss in Africa will come to know your truth and be set free to praise your name. Amen.

ABOUT DAVID COFFEY

David Coffey is the President of the Baptist World Alliance. He previously served as the pastor to three local churches in England and as General Secretary of the Baptist Union of Great Britain. During his international ministry David has visited over 75 countries in all the continents but has a particular interest in the Middle East and seeks to strengthen the work and witness of the churches there. He and his wife Janet have two adult children and four grandchildren. David is a member of the Torch Council of Reference.

ALL GOD'S CHILDREN: Hospitable

1 Peter 4:8–11

Above all, love each other deeply, because love covers over a multitude of sins. Offer hospitality to one another without grumbling. Each of you should use whatever gift you have received to serve others, as faithful stewards of God's grace in its various forms. If you speak, you should do so as one who speaks the very words of God. If you serve, you should do so with the strength God provides, so that in all things God may be praised through Jesus Christ. To him be the glory and the power for ever and ever. Amen.

Michele Guinness writes

Living in Coventry during the Hindu festival of Divali was such fun. I was inundated with invitations to eat in our neighbours' homes, and will never forget those curries, chapattis and onion bhajis – so much better than any I had ever eaten in an Indian restaurant.

But it was a real challenge too. When did I ever invite my Hindu or Muslim neighbours in for a meal at Christian festivals? And what could I offer them in the way of traditional food, earning the right to explain what my faith meant to me, and why my home was a centre of Christian celebration?

Offer hospitality, Peter says. And without grumbling or resentment. Never mind the incursion into our busy lives, the planning, the shopping, the chopping, the cooking and the mounds of washing up afterwards. Never

> **Offering hospitality to neighbours is a discipline, but a real blessing too**

mind if our offerings are underdone, overcooked or look like the garden compost. Love makes up for any lack.

But if we are a 'Delia' or a 'Jamie', then we could use that gift to God's glory, as a way of serving strangers. You never know when you might be entertaining an angel, says the writer to the Hebrews.

When I was baptised and rejected by family, my church was thrilled to see a Jewish girl come to Christ. Yet no one invited me for a meal or adopted me as part of their family. Instead of grumbling about my loneliness, I invited them to my tiny little bedsit, and made some lasting friendships. Offering hospitality to neighbours is a discipline, but a real blessing too.

PRAISE

Thank you, Lord, for the many openings given to Torch Trust to show love and compassion to people with sight loss in this country and around the world. May all those contacts be characterised by Christian hospitality.

REFLECT

As you play your recording or radio today, reflect on how many times you have grumbled about your neighbours – particularly those who are immigrants. It's so easy to adopt the critical habits of others. In what ways could you show them Christian love and hospitality?

PRAY

Father, help me to show your love and concern to others by being involved in mission both on my own doorstep and around the world. Amen.

ABOUT MICHELE GUINNESS

Brought up in a practising Jewish family, Michele became a Christian and went on to marry a Church of England minister. She worked in the UK media, and for two years presented her own daily lunchtime programme on BBC local radio. She became Head of Communications for the NHS in Cumbria and Lancashire, but now concentrates on writing, training and speaking all over the UK. She has written eleven best-selling books, including her autobiography, *Chosen*.

ALL GOD'S CHILDREN: Family

EPHESIANS 3:14–19

For this reason I kneel before the Father, from whom every family in heaven and on earth derives its name. I pray that out of his glorious riches he may strengthen you with power through his Spirit in your inner being, so that Christ may dwell in your hearts through faith. And I pray that you, being rooted and established in love, may have power, together with all the Lord's people, to grasp how wide and long and high and deep is the love of Christ, and to know this love that surpasses knowledge – that you may be filled to the measure of all the fullness of God.

RONA GIBB WRITES

How amazing it is to realise that we are all part of God's family! In his letter to the Ephesian believers, Paul prays that they may be able to grasp the wonder and privilege of this position, as well as praying that they will live lives that demonstrate their family likeness to God the Father in Christ. We are in God's family only because of Christ's great love; we were so precious to him that he bought us the gift of life by his death on the cross.

Being part of God's family brings both privileges and responsibilities. Our privileges include the wonderful fact that nothing can separate us from God's love, not even death; our place in his family is secure for eternity. Our responsibilities mean that we need to be constantly living in the power of God's love. We have the opportunity to be constantly filled with God's Holy Spirit, and the first

> ... it is God's will that we are ... enabled by his Spirit to show his love to people around us

fruit he bears is love. This must be directed not only towards God but also to our brothers and sisters in Christ.

Within any family, people are recognised by their likeness to each other. Children resemble their parents; and it is God's will that we are constantly being changed into his likeness, changed by his love, and enabled by his Spirit to show his love to people around us who largely have no time for God. So Paul urges us to 'live a life worthy of Christ's calling.'

PRAISE

Lord, I'm so glad for the rich diversity in the world you have created. I rejoice in it! But I'm also glad for the points of contact, for the things I can find in common with others from around the world.

REFLECT

While you play your international music or voices, try to make a mental list of the differences from that which you hear on local radio and on the streets in your community. Are the instruments or chords or harmonies strange to you? And what similarities can you hear?

PRAY

Bless, dear Lord, the partnerships Torch Trust has with other organisations and Christian missions around the world, such as Compass Braille and United Bible Societies. Together may they work in harmony for the benefit of many with sight loss. Amen.

ABOUT RONA GIBB

Rona, who has had very little sight since birth, studied at London Bible College and then worked for Torch during the 1970s, where she met Tony. They married and went to India from 1978 to 1985, establishing India Fellowship for the Visually Handicapped whose aim is encouraging the Church to integrate people with sight loss. Returning to England, Rona and Tony set up Compass Braille, which produces braille Bibles and booklets in over 40 languages. Rona is now a Torch trustee.

ALL GOD'S CHILDREN: Loving

1 John 4:7–12; 5:2–4

Dear friends, let us love one another, for love comes from God. Everyone who loves has been born of God and knows God. Whoever does not love does not know God, because God is love. This is how God showed his love among us: He sent his one and only Son into the world that we might live through him. This is love: not that we loved God, but that he loved us and sent his Son as an atoning sacrifice for our sins. Dear friends, since God so loved us, we also ought to love one another. No one has ever seen God; but if we love one another, God lives in us and his love is made complete in us.

…This is how we know that we love the children of God: by loving God and carrying out his commands. In fact, this is love for God: to keep his commands. And his commands are not burdensome, for everyone born of God overcomes the world.

Curtis Lee Hall writes

Who are God's children? How should they act in this world? And what is their goal?

As God's children, we must learn to love as he does, keeping his commandments and doing no wrong to our neighbour. As we daily pick up our cross and abide in him, his love will be manifested through us. Apart from him, we can do nothing. But as we learn to abide in him, he can live and love through us – and the world will know we are his disciples.

Much of the world thinks Christianity is a bunch of harsh rules and commandments saying 'do not do this' or 'do not do that'. Most do not understand that the violation of God's commandments or 'do nots' is the very thing that brings the suffering, the pain, the hatred and even death into their lives. We, as children of God, need to show the world that the love of God is the answer for all this suffering and pain, that sin is the enemy of their soul, and that God has a redemptive plan to bring us out of all sin and into his glorious kingdom of love.

Remember, children of God: without love we are nothing. Love is our goal, with an attitude of no compromise in regards to sin.

> Remember, children of God: without love we are nothing

REFLECT

As you come to prayer today, why not sing any song of praise to God for the love he has shown to you? Perhaps you know the simple chorus by Alison Huntley which goes: 'Thank you, Jesus, thank you, Jesus, thank you, Lord, for loving me' (© 1978 Kingsway's Thankyou Music). If you have internet access you could play it on YouTube.

PRAISE

I offer you praise, O God, for all the donations, both financial and material, which mean that Torch Trust is able to work internationally with people who are blind or partially sighted.

PRAY

Lord, help me to make Christian love my goal in all my relationships with others. Amen.

ABOUT CURTIS LEE HALL

Curtis lives in Washington, USA. He became totally blind in 1998 when he was in his late twenties. At present, Curtis is a single father with two children, a daughter Arielle and a son Noah. Curtis enjoys reading literature from the Torch Library, especially biographies and autobiographies. He loves to communicate with people all over the world by email and through his website.

ALL GOD'S CHILDREN: Rich

DEUTERONOMY 8:17–20; LUKE 12:32

You may say to yourself, 'My power and the strength of my hands have produced this wealth for me.' But remember the LORD your God, for it is he who gives you the ability to produce wealth, and so confirms his covenant, which he swore to your ancestors, as it is today.

'If you ever forget the LORD your God and follow other gods and worship and bow down to them, I testify against you today that you will surely be destroyed. Like the nations the LORD destroyed before you, so you will be destroyed for not obeying the LORD your God.'

…Do not be afraid, little flock, for your Father has been pleased to give you the kingdom.

WINSTON CHIDZAMBUYO WRITES

One day while I was in my home village, a Christian brother said to me, 'God does not favour me. See how poor I am.' Such sayings are becoming very common in Malawi. Some people think that if they are poor their relationship with God is wrong in some way. Others will advise them to do something to gain God's favour. They limit God's riches to monetary terms only.

In a good number of churches and prayer meetings, I have heard people praying for material wealth above their other needs, basing their argument on our Lord's promises. Many people have misunderstood Jesus' words by limiting his promises to material wealth, forgetting that the Lord opened the door wide for us to ask for anything according to his riches: 'Do not be afraid, little flock, for your Father has been pleased to give you the kingdom.'

Most people – unfortunately including some Christians – forget the simple fact that it is God who gives wealth and that it is not gained by our wisdom or strength. God gives or opens the door for wealth to those he wishes, by his grace. What we have to do is to seek his kingdom and righteousness first.

Christians are a very blessed and rich people and should remember that his wishes for us are far better than ours.

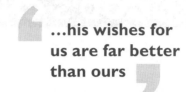

...his wishes for us are far better than ours

PRAISE

Thank you, Father, that — whatever my material circumstances — I am rich because of your love for me.

REFLECT

N*kosi sikelel' iAfrika* is the rousing South African anthem which gained popularity during the struggle against Apartheid. Can you remember and hum the tune? One English translation of the opening verse is:

God bless Africa
May her glory be lifted high
Hear our petitions
God bless us, your children.

PRAY

Lord, often people with sight loss are the poorest of the poor in many developing countries. Help Torch Trust distribute aid wisely and multiply its effects so that families facing starvation and homelessness can be fed and housed. Amen.

ABOUT WINSTON CHIDZAMBUYO

Winston first heard about Torch when co-founders Ron and Stella Heath visited Malawi. He met them again in 1991, this time inviting them to his house for supper where they explained to him about the ministry of Torch Trust. He was touched by the plight of blind and partially sighted people in Malawi. When he was asked to join the Board of Trustees there, he says he 'gladly accepted'. He served in several roles and since 2004 has been the national administrator.

ALL GOD'S CHILDREN: Thirsty

ISAIAH 41:17; PSALM 63:1

The poor and needy search for water,
    but there is none;
    their tongues are parched with thirst.
    But I the LORD will answer them;
    I, the God of Israel, will not forsake them.

…You, God, are my God,
    earnestly I seek you;
    I thirst for you,
    my whole being longs for you,
    in a dry and parched land
    where there is no water.

JANET STAFFORD WRITES

Ah, the smell of the rain as it sweeps in great visible waves across the Shire Valley of Malawi after months of drought!

The ground is cracked and barren; everything is brown in the dry season months. Day after day the sun beats down relentlessly, the heat is unbearable and the longing is for rain. Then one day the rain can be heard coming from a distance, which causes great excitement and expectancy. As the first rain falls on the dry earth, the smell rises – it's the most wonderful smell because it's the smell of knowing that at last the dry season is coming to an end.

This is my most indelible Africa smell. No matter where I have been in Africa, I always long for that smell.

In a spiritual sense, too, there is often within us that longing that the rain of the Holy Spirit will come to revive and refresh the dry and parched places of our lives. The heat and pressure of our circumstances affect our lives; we become dry and withered inside. We wait with expectancy and longing. The rain of the Holy Spirit comes. As it falls on our souls and we absorb it into our beings, the response is a sweet smell that rises up to the nostrils of God. Today, are you feeling parched and dry? Listen, the rain *is* coming.

> **...there is often within us that longing that the rain of the Holy Spirit will come to revive and refresh the dry and parched places of our lives**

REFLECT

As you play your world music for the last time this week, imagine that smell of the rains on the parched African dust, as Janet describes. Is there a smell that you welcome and enjoy as much as Africans love that smell after drought? The first cup of coffee of the morning? Fresh-baked bread? How much do you long for God's blessing?

PRAISE

Thank you, Father, for the experience of your blessing, which is like fresh rain after a drought.

PRAY

I pray for all the Torch staff who either visit or are based outside the UK, that they will have your compassion for those with sight loss and your wisdom to know how best to use limited resources to bless them. Amen.

ABOUT JANET STAFFORD

Janet and her husband Michael have been involved in Torch Trust for over 20 years. Janet serves as International Leader, reaching out with encouragement to blind people all over the world. In particular, she is regularly involved in extended visits to Torch Trust in Malawi, where she visits blind people in their villages, giving support and encouragement. Janet and Michael have two adult children, one of whom is involved in church planting in South Africa.

WEEK 7

VISION

Torch Trust describes itself as 'a Christian organisation with a worldwide vision for people with sight loss.'

What is that vision? It's that blind and partially sighted people around the world can have equal access to the gospel of Jesus Christ through the Bible, Christian literature and Christian fellowship, and be accepted into church life on equal terms with sighted people; a vision to see those with sight loss fulfilled and included. Though expressed in a few words, it's a huge vision – but then, we have a powerful God.

ENCOURAGEMENT

'This whole undertaking was God's, not ours. It was too big for us to handle anyway. If he could create beauty and order out of chaos in the universe, it was a light thing for him to help us!'

From Where There Is Vision (1981) by Stella Heath

'One day the Lord will return in glory … Until that great day, it is our prayer that the Torch Family will follow the path which has been shown us and that, as a result, many people struggling with blindness of body or heart, may find the Light of Life.'

from Coping With The Camel (1996) by Stella Heath

 The most pathetic person in the world is someone who has sight, but has no vision.
– Helen Keller, who was deafblind

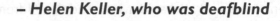

'When Torch House moved from Hallaton to Market Harborough, we brought with us some well-worn smooth stones from the Hallaton grounds, stones which represented a familiar and comfortable path. We then found some rough stones from the site of the new building, symbolic of an unfamiliar path which would, in time, become smooth and homely. These two sets of stones have been cemented into a wooden cross which hangs in the conference room of Torch House – the room in which we start each day with prayer – and serve as a memorial to God's faithfulness as we serve the vision he has given us, just as God gave instructions to Joshua and his people to set up a memorial of stones after the crossing of the Jordan.

Torch staff member

 Faith is to believe what you do not yet see; the reward for this faith is to see what you believe.

– Saint Augustine, influential bishop
of the early Church

MULTI-SENSORY FOCUS

'The least movement is of importance to all nature. The entire ocean is affected by a pebble.' So wrote Blaise Pascal (1623-1662). Anyone with vision understands the inter-connectedness of everything in the plan of God.

This week, try to find two stones – a smooth stone or pebble and a rough stone – to add extra meaning to your prayer and reading.

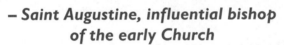

THIS WEEK'S CONTRIBUTORS

MARILYN BAKER • REV'D MIKE ENDICOTT • SHEILA ARMSTRONG • STELLA HEATH
REV'D DR STEVE BRADY • SUSAN RICHARDS • ANDREW NICHOLSON

VISION: God's plan for you

JEREMIAH 29:11–14

'For I know the plans I have for you,' declares the LORD, 'plans to prosper you and not to harm you, plans to give you hope and a future. Then you will call on me and come and pray to me, and I will listen to you. You will seek me and find me when you seek me with all your heart. I will be found by you,' declares the LORD, 'and will bring you back from captivity. I will gather you from all the nations and places where I have banished you,' declares the LORD, 'and will bring you back to the place from which I carried you into exile.'

MARILYN BAKER WRITES

Jeremiah 29:11 was the inspiration for one of the songs that
I have written:

God has a plan for you, something only you can do,
You are so valuable to him.
You are beyond compare, a priceless jewel so very rare,
He gave just everything to make you his own.

> *God wants just you, yes, no one else will do.*
> *Listen to him call you by name.*
> *You were in his plan before the world began,*
> *And he longs that you live your life for him.*

He knows the power of sin, the struggles that you have within,
His love just longs to set you free.
And as you open up your heart, and give to him every part,
He'll make you all you long to be.

God has no other way of spreading his love today,
To those who live in so much need,
Than using those who belong to him, who are ready to give
    him everything,
So he can live and speak through them.

> **You were in his plan before the world began,**
>
> **And he longs that you live your life for him.**

REFLECT

Under the influence of the weather and the waves, any rough stone on a beach may end up smooth. But it will never become an exact copy of another smooth stone. As you run your fingers over your rough and smooth stones be assured that, whatever your circumstances, God has a unique plan for you! You are never just another pebble on the beach. You are unique and precious in his sight, handpicked for his purposes.

PRAISE

Father God, I praise you for all who glimpse a vision from you and strive to fulfil it. Thank you for Ron and Stella Heath and their obedience to the vision you gave them for people with sight loss which was fulfilled in Torch Trust.

PRAY

Guide me, Father, to know what you want me to do for you. Amen.

ABOUT MARILYN BAKER

At God's leading, Marilyn gave up her job as a music teacher and started an itinerant music ministry. She travelled extensively and became for a while Britain's top female gospel singer. Marilyn Baker Ministries continues to bless many thousands of people each year. In partnership with Tracy Williamson, Marilyn undertakes church encouragement weekends, workshops, conferences, ministering to the elderly and visiting prisons. Marilyn has been a user of Torch Library services for many years. She is currently chair of Torch trustees and the presenter of Torch's weekly 'Insight' programme on Premier Christian Radio.

VISION: Trusting and jumping

2 KINGS 6:15–17

When the servant of the man of God got up and went out early the next morning, an army with horses and chariots had surrounded the city. 'Oh no, my lord! What shall we do?' the servant asked.

'Don't be afraid,' the prophet answered. 'Those who are with us are more than those who are with them.'

And Elisha prayed, 'Open his eyes, LORD, so that he may see.' Then the LORD opened the servant's eyes, and he looked and saw the hills full of horses and chariots of fire all around Elisha.

MIKE ENDICOTT WRITES

Life can be full of visions, dreams and plans. Many of us are always wondering about the world being a better place – if only we could…

Our single greatest problem is this: the enemy arranged against us seems too big! We get daunted by the problems and don't focus on God's strength to overcome them. We know the worldly practicalities and forget to focus on the truths of the kingdom. Other people, their traditions and their views, can all seem set against us.

But if God has given us a vision, a big idea, a way forward, then no matter how impossible it looks, we can start to do it anyway!

Success is born out of trust – trust in God. One picture of trust is of us standing on the end of a high diving board, looking down into an empty swimming pool. How do we feel? At the

Divine grace and support are attracted by the sight of our trusting

other end of the pool stands the Caretaker. We shout out to him, 'Mr Caretaker, fill up the pool for me, I want to jump!' But the Caretaker shakes his head at us and says, 'No, you jump, and I'll fill the pool!'

Whether or not we can see how our plans and visions for the future are going to work is irrelevant to heaven's grace. Divine grace and support are attracted by the sight of our trusting. It is our trust that pulls God's reality into ours. Whatever it is, if you believe it is from God, then go for it!

PRAISE

Thank you, Father, for the continuing vision of the trustees and those in leadership of Torch Trust, as they take the work forward in challenging times.

REFLECT

Taking the stones in your hand, which one feels most like you? Are you more like the rough stone or the smooth one? Or are you a mix of the two? How different would you like that to be; in other words, what is the vision for your life? And what needs to happen to bring about your vision?

PRAY

Give me more faith, dear Lord, to step out with courage into the future I believe you have called me to. Amen.

ABOUT MIKE ENDICOTT

Mike is an Anglican clergyman and author living in South Wales. He is one of the founders of 'The Well Centre', the administrative focus for the Order of Jacob's Well. The Order was founded by a group of lay and ordained people involved in Christian healing (www.jacobswell.org.uk).

VISION: Changing the world

GENESIS 39:19–23

When his master heard the story his wife told him, saying, 'This is how your slave treated me,' he burned with anger. Joseph's master took him and put him in prison, the place where the king's prisoners were confined.

But while Joseph was there in the prison, the LORD was with him; he showed him kindness and granted him favour in the eyes of the prison warden. So the warden put Joseph in charge of all those held in the prison, and he was made responsible for all that was done there. The warden paid no attention to anything under Joseph's care, because the LORD was with Joseph and gave him success in whatever he did.

ANDREW NICHOLSON WRITES

Joseph had spent two years in prison on false charges, with no immediate prospect of release. Coupled with the (later) disappointment of being forgotten by the one man (the chief cupbearer) who could have spoken up for him, would you have expected Joseph to have had any vision? Any hope? Any prospects?

Were his two dreams, indicating that one day he would rule over his parents and brothers, just a distant memory? Did he think God had forgotten him? Abandoned him?

Yet we read, and not for the first time, that 'the Lord was with him' and 'gave him success in whatever he did.'

American businessman and leadership expert Joel A Barker wrote, 'Vision without action is

> **Vision doesn't belong only to those who are exceptionally gifted...**

merely a dream. Action without vision just passes the time. Vision with action can change the world.'

Joseph was hardly in a position to act on his vision – or so he thought! Yet a vision that extended to just a limited circle of people, in a place that Joseph would not have chosen to be, with restricted scope for his activities, was still blessed by God.

Vision doesn't belong only to those who are exceptionally gifted or who have incredible foresight of mind. It is something within reach of those who, like Joseph, shun sin, remain faithful to God, use the gifts God has given them and are diligent in whatever they do. Oh, and who also seize the opportunities that God, in his providence, sends their way!

Why not start today, with God's help, to change the world?

REFLECT

Both rough and smooth times in your life can contribute to your vision of God's plan for you. With your stones in your hands, think about how the different experiences of your life have given you understanding of the Lord's purposes for you. If you feel uncertain of his calling on your life, why not ask him to show you?

PRAISE

Thank you, dear Lord, that my times are in your hands.

PRAY

Father, guide the future of all areas of Torch ministry. Grow the work by your Holy Spirit, to bless many more thousands of people with sight loss. Amen.

ABOUT ANDREW NICHOLSON

Andrew is Assistant Chief Executive of Torch Trust. After working in banking for 19 years, he became a pastor of an FIEC church in 1996, followed in 2001 by time as Event Manager for FIEC, culminating in the Cheltenham Bible Festival in 2007. Being involved with Torch Trust through the festival planning, living in Market Harborough and hearing of their need for senior administrative and financial help, the step to his current role was seen as God's leading and provision.

VISION: Recognising his voice

PSALM 123:2

As the eyes of slaves look to the hand of their master,
    as the eyes of a female slave look to the hand of her mistress,
    so our eyes look to the LORD our God,
    till he shows us his mercy.

SHEILA ARMSTRONG WRITES

My guide dog, Mist, was famous as a puppy for recognising many hand signals. But only a few signals and commands are actually needed for guiding so, as her training progressed, life became much simpler and less confusing for her. By the time she started guiding me, she'd learned all she needed to know. But when I spoke the simple commands, she didn't pick up on them straight away. She had to get used to my voice.

But now, her eyes and her ears are on me. She watches my hand for a quick flick right or left where we have a choice of two directions; she watches my feet too, as I get them into position for 'forward', 'back', 'right' or 'left'; and she listens to my voice as I speak the few easy commands she's learned to obey.

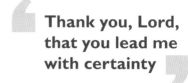

Thank you, Lord, that you lead me with certainty

When we first make Jesus Lord of our lives, we do want to please him but we don't always recognise his voice. The more we read his Word and learn of his ways, the easier this becomes.

Of course, there are times when Mist hears or sees me perfectly well but feels like ignoring me and doing something else! Then I work hard to regain her attention and obedience, especially where there could be danger.

I'm so glad that the Lord leads me with certainty. He draws me close and shows mercy when I turn back to him.

REFLECT

Taking the rough stone in your hand, can you recall a time you either just did what you wanted to or ignored what the Lord said? What did it feel like? From time to time we all choose our way instead of the Lord's way. Sheila tells us that when her guide dog ignores her she 'works hard to regain Mist's attention and obedience'. Is there a lesson there about the Lord's actions toward you when you go astray?

PRAISE

Thank you, Father, for the wise counsel of the trustees in keeping Torch Trust close to your will; and for the willing work of many volunteers who help at Torch House, Torch Holiday & Retreat Centre and in Torch Fellowship Groups across the country.

PRAY

Help me, O Lord, to recognise your voice and to resist temptation to go my own way. Amen.

ABOUT SHEILA ARMSTRONG

The magazines Sheila found at blind school in Edinburgh made her curious about Torch Trust. As she says, 'Having worked with Torch for 33 years, I now have some idea!' Sheila began by collating page after page of braille; then moved to magazine work – brailling and typing scripts in the days before computers. 'When computers took us by storm, I took over working with volunteers to produce library books and other material in braille and giant print,' says Sheila. 'The Torch Library would be nowhere without our volunteers!'

VISION: In the storm

Mark 4:35,37–41

That day when evening came, he said to his disciples, 'Let us go over to the other side.'

…A furious squall came up, and the waves broke over the boat, so that it was nearly swamped. Jesus was in the stern, sleeping on a cushion. The disciples woke him and said to him, 'Teacher, don't you care if we drown?'

He got up, rebuked the wind and said to the waves, 'Quiet! Be still!' Then the wind died down and it was completely calm.

He said to his disciples, 'Why are you so afraid? Do you still have no faith?'

They were terrified and asked each other, 'Who is this? Even the wind and the waves obey him!'

Steve Brady writes

It had been a long day of teaching and Jesus, understandably tired, left the crowd and joined a boatful of his disciples on the Galilee. Before falling asleep, he gave directions to cross to the other side. Suddenly, a life-threatening storm engulfed them – and Jesus slept on! In their despair, they awakened him with a note of accusation, 'Don't you care if we drown?'

In times of extreme trial, when life may seem so unfair, it is tempting to assume the worst about the Lord. Perhaps, in their naivety, the disciples assumed that having Jesus on board was a cast iron guarantee that storms would bypass them. Yet, nowhere are we promised that Christ's presence will always keep us *from* life's challenges. Rather, Christ's promise is to keep us *through* them.

> **Real faith trusts what the Master says**

Jesus ignores their reproof and immediately stills the storm, following up with an intriguing double question: 'Why are you so afraid? Do you still have no faith?' Why this question about faith? Because, Jesus had said, 'Let's go to the other side.' Real faith trusts what the Master says. In its widest application, Jesus intends to take all his frightened and bedraggled disciples to 'the other side' – eternal life – and meanwhile be with them on the journey. Are you facing a crisis today, wondering if the Lord really cares? Sadly, it is often easier to tremble than to trust. Will it be fear or faith today? It's your choice – panic or prayer! Trust him – he'll see you *through*.

PRAISE

Of course even the winds and waves obey you, Father! Thank you that this story from the Bible reminds me of your tremendous power – a power that's more than enough to help me through the storms of my life.

REFLECT

Today Steve encourages us to trust Jesus when we're in a storm. Let your rough stone bring to mind a storm you have been through – or are going through right now. Are you the kind of person who trembles or trusts? Do you panic or pray? Ask the Lord to strengthen your faith so that you can trust him to keep you through life's challenges.

PRAY

Sovereign God, please be with all blind and partially sighted people who live alone and who feel overwhelmed by life's storms. Bring many more into contact with Torch so that they can find fellowship and encouragement. Amen.

ABOUT STEVE BRADY

Steve was born and educated in Liverpool where he was converted in his teens. He trained at what is now the London School of Theology where he met Brenda, his wife of over 30 years. They have two children and three grandchildren. He serves as principal of Moorlands College, is a trustee of the Keswick Convention and chair of the Association of Bible College Principals. Steve is also the author of several books and a member of the Torch Council of Reference.

VISION: Beyond tears

REVELATION 21:3,4; 22:3–5

And I heard a loud voice from the throne saying, 'Look! God's dwelling place is now among the people, and he will dwell with them. They will be his people, and God himself will be with them and be their God. He will wipe every tear from their eyes. There will be no more death or mourning or crying or pain, for the old order of things has passed away.'

… There will be no more night. They will not need the light of a lamp or the light of the sun, for the Lord God will give them light. And they will reign for ever and ever.

… No longer will there be any curse. The throne of God and of the Lamb will be in the city, and his servants will serve him. They will see his face, and his name will be on their foreheads. There will be no more night. They will not need the light of a lamp or the light of the sun, for the Lord God will give them light. And they will reign for ever and ever.

SUSAN RICHARDS WRITES

The book of Revelation pulls back the curtains, allowing the believer a thrilling glimpse into the splendour of heaven.

God's presence These Bible verses give an emphatic three-fold promise of God's continual presence with his people: he will be among them, he will dwell with them and he himself will be with them and be their God. Even our deepest moments of fellowship with him on earth are tainted by sin; this new intimacy will surpass them all.

God's provision With breathtaking tenderness we see our holy, majestic God stooping to wipe the tear-stained faces of his children. Our sorrows will be gone, never to return. God will also provide all the light we need, for he himself is the light. No lesser illumination from lamp or even the sun in its radiance will be required. Never again will we stumble or miss our way; no lurking shadow of doubt will remain.

Heaven's permanence

Relationships on earth are ripped apart by death. A loved one is gone; the pain unbearable. God's family in heaven fears no such severance, for we will reign with Christ for ever and ever.

> **Our sorrows then will be gone, never to return**

Is sorrow threatening to overwhelm your aching heart? Are you smarting from the sting of separation? Stretch out your hand of faith to catch the vision of heaven – 'No more death or mourning, crying or pain, for those whose hope is anchored in Christ.' Hallelujah!

PRAISE

Father, I give you thanks for all the relationships with other Christian and organisations for the blind and partially sighted that Torch has developed over the years. Bless their cooperation together.

REFLECT

Pick up your smooth stone and reflect on the flawlessness of heaven, giving thanks that one day you will experience its perfection. Earthly circumstances are temporary. Take fresh hope from the certainty of heaven.

PRAY

May the reality of heaven invade my life on earth, giving me hope and joy right now as well as unshakeable future security. Amen.

ABOUT SUSAN RICHARDS

Susan (www.susanrichards.org) worked for eight years as Regional Secretary for Torch in the 1970s and now, with her husband Peter, is actively involved with the Torch Fellowship Group in Falmouth, Cornwall. Susan is an author and reviews articles for a number of Torch magazines.

VISION: Fruit in old age

Psalm 92:12–15

The righteous will flourish like a palm tree,
    they will grow like a cedar of Lebanon;

planted in the house of the Lord,
    they will flourish in the courts of our God.

They will still bear fruit in old age,
    they will stay fresh and green,

proclaiming, 'The Lord is upright;
    he is my Rock, and there is no wickedness in him.'

Stella Heath writes

Spring had come early and the poet Wordsworth would have been delighted with the 'host of golden daffodils' which covered the grassy slopes under the trees. But now they were all dying, faded, drooping and unattractive. I felt a little like that myself. To what purpose is my life? What use have I been? A great sadness came over me – I felt old!

Just beside me was a mass of white pear blossom trained up the wall. The bees were having a wonderful time, landing on flower after flower, happily gathering their nectar, quite unaware of the way their bodies were distributing pollen from one flower to another. That pollination was so necessary, for without it the tree would not grow any fruit.

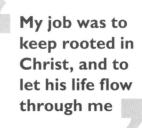

My job was to keep rooted in Christ, and to let his life flow through me

'Look more closely.' I recognised the voice of the Lord. With sudden delight I saw he had something to say to me. 'Look at the trunk of the pear tree.' I looked down under the flower-laden branches. I was amazed to see a gnarled, twisted old trunk which looked 'past it'. But it was feeding each flower on the branches, supplying the life which the tree needed to be fruitful.

I learned a lesson that day. I might be old, 'past my sell-by date', but still alert mentally and I had a very important task still to do. My job was to keep rooted in Christ, and to let his life flow through me. (Taken from an article written for *Torch Family News*)

REFLECT

What makes the rough stone smooth? In the natural, the rough stone becomes smooth through the action of rubbing constantly against others. In our spiritual lives, it's often the action of God and other people which enables us to fulfill our vision. God spoke to Stella Heath through the pear tree. How can you take time out of your routine today to enable God to speak to you about his plans for you?

PRAISE

Dear God, how blessed I am that you want to communicate with me and help me become all that I should be. Speak to me today. And help me to hear you.

PRAY

Father, encourage those with sight loss who are feeling 'past it' to know they are precious to you and still have a part to play in your plans. Amen.

ABOUT STELLA HEATH

Stella and Ron Heath were an ordinary couple who opened up their home to many young blind people. They shared the good news of Jesus with them. God gave them a vision to meet the needs of those with sight loss for accessible Christian resources and for fellowship. Later they felt called by God to extend the ministry of Torch Trust into countries around the world. Ron Heath died in 1999 and Stella in 2009 just as this book was about to go to press.

VISION: Pressing on, looking ahead

Philippians 3:10–14

I want to know Christ – yes, to know the power of his resurrection and participation in his sufferings, becoming like him in his death, and so, somehow, attaining to the resurrection from the dead.

Not that I have already obtained all this, or have already arrived at my goal, but I press on to take hold of that for which Christ Jesus took hold of me. Brothers and sisters, I do not consider myself yet to have taken hold of it. But one thing I do: Forgetting what is behind and straining toward what is ahead, I press on toward the goal to win the prize for which God has called me heavenward in Christ Jesus.

Dr Gordon Temple, CEO of Torch Trust, writes

Many people see Christians as backward-looking – wistfully remembering a golden age, perhaps a time when everyone went to church or when the Bible was more respected. Not so. We are people of the future.

Yes, we do look back, especially to the death and resurrection of Jesus, but we do so to get our bearings for our onward journey. We may reflect on God's leading in our lives and give thanks for his blessing but we shouldn't live in the past. We are citizens of the kingdom of heaven and we are to be focused on bringing it in.

Without Jesus, thinking about what lies ahead is no more than speculation. The relationship we have with Jesus assures us of our ultimate future, guaranteed by his own resurrection. But equally assured is a share in his sufferings. Maturity in Christian life holds these two truths together: we press on toward our future reality *with Jesus* while living positively *with Jesus* in our present reality.

This series of readings has been published to celebrate Torch Trust's golden jubilee. Behind are 50 years of growth and blessing for which we thank God. Ahead is uncharted territory for which we trust God. The best is yet to come! We *live by faith, not by sight* (2 Corinthians 5:7).

It's time to press on.

PRAISE AND PRAY:

FOR BLESSING PAST, PRESENT AND FUTURE

The Torch family marked the fiftieth anniversary of the founding of the work with a day of prayer on June 8 2009 at Torch house and at the Torch Holiday & Retreat Centre. Supporters and former staff members were able to link up with Torch House in a telephone conference. A tree was planted in the grounds, and this prayer of blessing read over it:

Father God, as we plant this tree, we are reminded that Torch is rooted in you, belongs to you, is dependent on you.

We pray that both the tree and the work of Torch Trust may grow, and grow as you direct.

As this tree extends its canopy, so may Torch reach out to more towns and cities in our land and to more places across the world.

As birds make nests in its branches, may people find in Torch a place of welcome and hospitality.

As people find shade and shelter under this tree, so may many find in Torch a place of fellowship.

As the tree produces fruit and seed, may Torch provide the resources that many need for full and whole lives of worship and service.

Lord, bless this tree. Bless the work of Torch Trust. Bless all who are associated with its work and ministry; in the name of the Father and of the Son and of the Holy Spirit. Amen.

Continued on the next page

Stella Heath, co-founder of Torch Trust, wrote in her book *Where There is Vision* (1981), 'Where we come to look into the way ahead and are asked about our future plans, we have to "roll up the map" and pray. We have been called to a walk of faith, and faith doesn't know the whole of the journey, but only the next step!'

Look back over the last 50 days. Thank the Lord for your journey; and ask him to help you trust him for the adventure of the next step.

PEACE WITH GOD

Maybe the Bible readings, reflections and prayers in this book have caused you to think about your own life and given you a desire to become a Christian and follow Jesus. You could use this prayer to begin your new life.

A PRAYER FOR FORGIVENESS AND FOR KNOWING PEACE AND ACCEPTANCE BY GOD

*Father in heaven, I know that I have done many wrong things
and that these things mean that there is a barrier between us.
I want to turn away from my past life and turn to you for forgiveness.
Please forgive me and help me not to do wrong again.
I believe that your Son Jesus Christ died for my sins,
was resurrected from the dead, is alive, hears my prayer
and wants to be close to me. I want to welcome Jesus into my life,
to become the Lord of my life and my Saviour from this day forward.
Send your Holy Spirit to help me live a new life,
obeying you and doing my best to understand your will
for the rest of my life. Amen.*

NEXT STEPS

The Bible says: **'If you declare with your mouth, "Jesus is Lord," and believe in your heart that God raised him from the dead, you will be saved. For it is with your heart that you believe and are justified, and it is with your mouth that you profess your faith and are saved.'** *(Romans 10:9,10)*

From the teaching of the Bible we learn that anyone praying this prayer with believing conviction becomes a child of God. A really good next thing to do, as it says in the verses above, is to find someone to tell about the step you have just taken.

Anyone who has committed themselves to following Jesus will know the joy of a clean and renewed life, a fresh start, the loving companionship of Jesus, the strengthening of the Holy Spirit and the peace of God.

THANK YOU

Thank you for your praying with us and for us. If you would like updated items for praise and prayer, call at any time on 01858 438277 or visit the Torch website (www.torchtrust.org) to find a daily prayer item and Bible text.

To keep you informed we would like to offer you our quarterly newsletter, *Torch Family News* with our *Daily Prayer Diary*. Please request these items in the medium that suits you (print, braille, audio or email) by calling 01858 438260 or emailing us (info@torchtrust.org).

If you have been challenged to think more about how people with sight loss can be made more welcome and more fully included within the life of your church, then visit www.torch-foursight.org and register for a free church pack of helpful resources.

TORCH TRUST PROVIDES

- **SCRIPTURE AND CHRISTIAN LITERATURE** in a range of accessible formats, made available through a free lending library, serving blind and partially sighted people across the UK and in 100 other countries

- **OUTREACH, SUPPORT AND BIBLE PORTIONS** in their own languages in accessible formats for blind and partially sighted people in Africa

- **WELCOME, FRIENDSHIP AND COMMUNITY** through 120 Torch Fellowship Groups around the UK

- **SPECIALIST HOLIDAYS AND RETREATS** led by experienced staff and volunteers

- **AWARENESS-RAISING AND TRAINING TO ENCOURAGE CHURCHES** to become more inclusive of people with sight loss

TORCH TRUST, Torch Way, Market Harborough, Leics. LE16 9HL
Tel: 01858 438260 Fax: 01858 438275
Email: info@torchtrust.org
Website: www.torchtrust.org
The Torch Trust for the Blind, registered charity no: 1095904

Torch Trust is a member of **Churches for All**, a partnership of Christian disability-focussed organisations seeking to enable the Church to be fully inclusive of disabled people: www.churchesforall.org.uk